West Flamborough Area in Colour Photos, Saving Our History One Photo at a Time

Photography
by Barbara Raué
©2022

Series Name: Cruising Ontario

Book 200: Freelton, Copetown, Crieff, Jerseyville, Lynden, Mountsberg, Puslinch, Strabane, West Flamborough

Cover photo: 14 Howell Road, Page 30

Series Name: Cruising Ontario
Saving Our History One Photo at a Time
in colour photos

Books Available in Alphabetical Order:
Aberfoyle, Acton, Alton, Amherstburg, Ancaster, Arthur, Auburn, Aylmer, Ayr, Beaver Valley, Belgrave, Belleville, Bloomingdale, Blyth, Brantford, Brockville, Burford, Burlington, Caledon, Caledonia, Cambridge, Carlow, Chatsworth, Clifford, Collingwood, Conestogo, Delhi, Dorchester to Aylmer, Drayton, Drumbo, Dundas, Dunlop, Eden Mills, Elmira, Elora, Erin, Essex, Fergus, Goderich, Grimsby, Guelph, Hagersville, Hamilton, Hanover, Harriston, Hespeler, Jarvis, Kingston, Kingsville, Kitchener, Lake Superior, Lincoln, Linwood, Listowel, London, Lucknow, Merrickville, Mono, Mount Forest, Mount Pleasant, Neustadt, New Hamburg, Newboro, Newport, Niagara-on-the-Lake, Oakville, Onondaga, Orangeville, Orillia, Owen Sound, Palmerston, Paris, Pelham, Perth, Peterborough, Petrolia, Port Colborne, Port Elgin, Portland, Preston, Rockwood, Sarnia, Sault Ste. Marie, Seaforth, Sheffield, Shelburne, Simcoe, Smiths Falls, Smithville, Southampton, St. Catharines, St. George, St. Jacobs, St. Marys, St. Thomas, Stoney Creek, Stratford, Thamesford, Thunder Bay, Tillsonburg, Toronto, Waterdown, Waterford, Waterloo, Welland, Wellesley, Westport, Windsor, Wingham, Woodstock

Visit Barbara's website to view all of her books
http://barbararaue.ca

Book 198: Chatsworth
Book 199: Wingham

Table of Contents

Freelton	Page 5
Concession 2	Page 18
Concession 4	Page 27
Copetown	Page 36
Crieff	Page 40
Jerseyville	Page 43
Lynden	Page 44
Mountsberg	Page 52
Puslinch	Page 57
Strabane	Page 58
West Flamborough	Page 63

Flamborough is a former municipality in the city of Hamilton. For most of its existence before amalgamation with Hamilton in 2001, Flamborough comprised the former townships of East Flamborough, West Flamborough, and Beverly, as well as the village of Waterdown. Other Flamborough communities include Carlisle, Christie's Corners, Clappison's Corners, Copetown, Freelton, Greensville, Lynden, Kirkwall, Millgrove, Mountsberg, Orkney, Peter's Corners, Rockton, Troy, Sheffield, Valens, and Westover.

After the American Revolution in 1783 and the creation of Upper Canada, land at the western end of Lake Ontario was surveyed and organized into townships, which included East Flamborough, West Flamborough and Beverly. Governor's Road (also known as Queen's Highway 99) was built on the border with neighboring Ancaster Township linking York (later Toronto) and London.

In 2001, the provincial government amalgamated Flamborough with Ancaster, Dundas, Glanbrook, Stoney Creek and Hamilton into the City of Hamilton.

Copetown is a rural neighborhood located east of Brantford. William Cope, a United Empire Loyalist from the state of New York settled here in 1794.

Jerseyville was initially settled by United Empire Loyalists from New Jersey in the late 1770s. The Brantford to Hamilton rail trail passes through Jerseyville in place of the old train tracks. The original Jerseyville train station building can be found at Westfield Heritage Village in Rockton.

There used to be a train station in Lynden that went to Hamilton. Currently Lynden has many farmers, small business entrepreneurs and commuters to Hamilton, Cambridge, Dundas, Brantford and Toronto.

Freelton

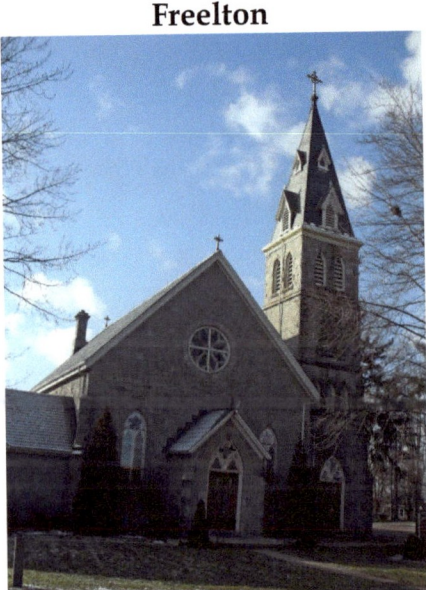

Our Lady of Carmel Roman Catholic Church – rose window, three-story tower

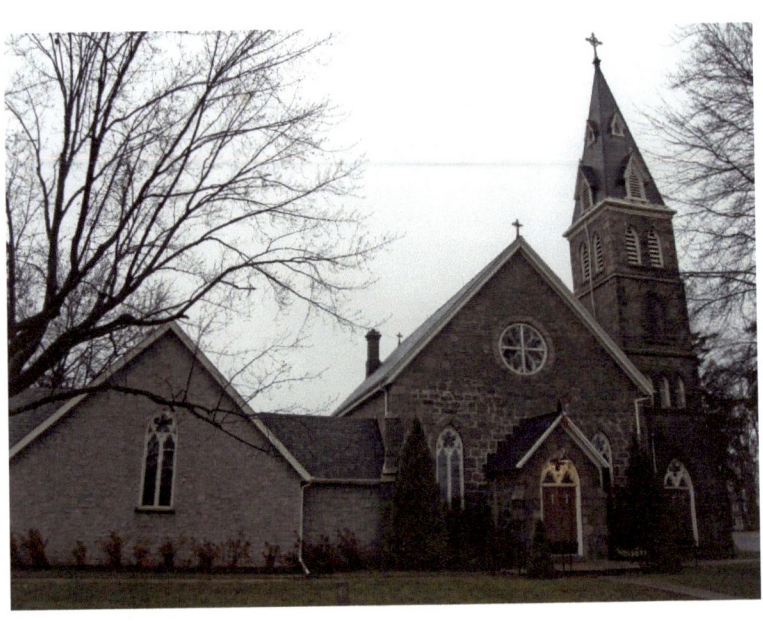

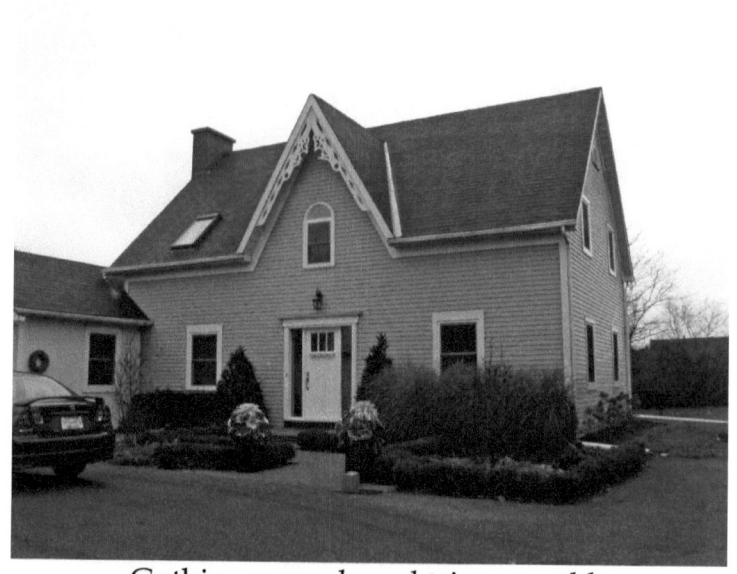

Gothic – verge board trim on gable

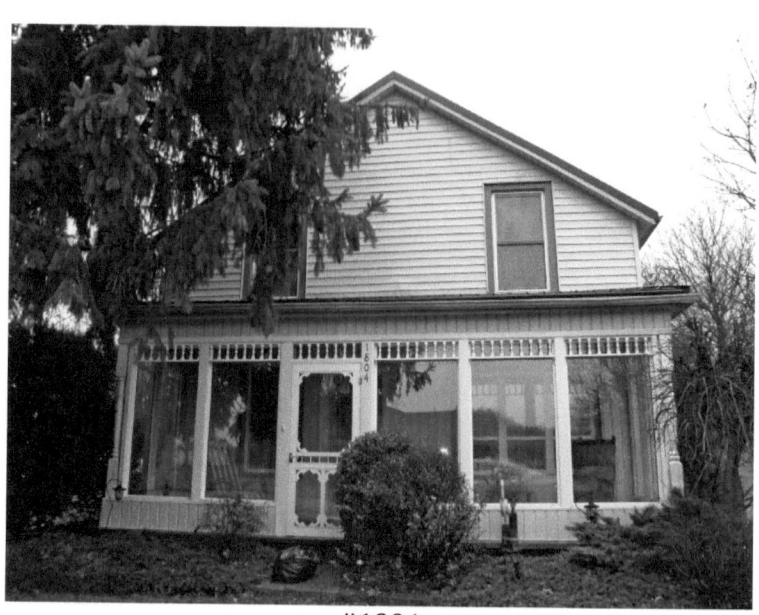

#1804

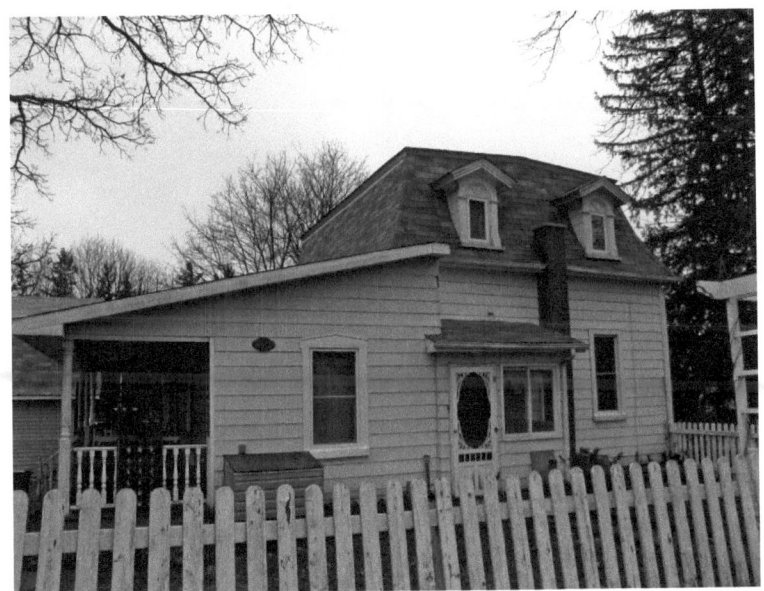

#1808 – dormers in roof

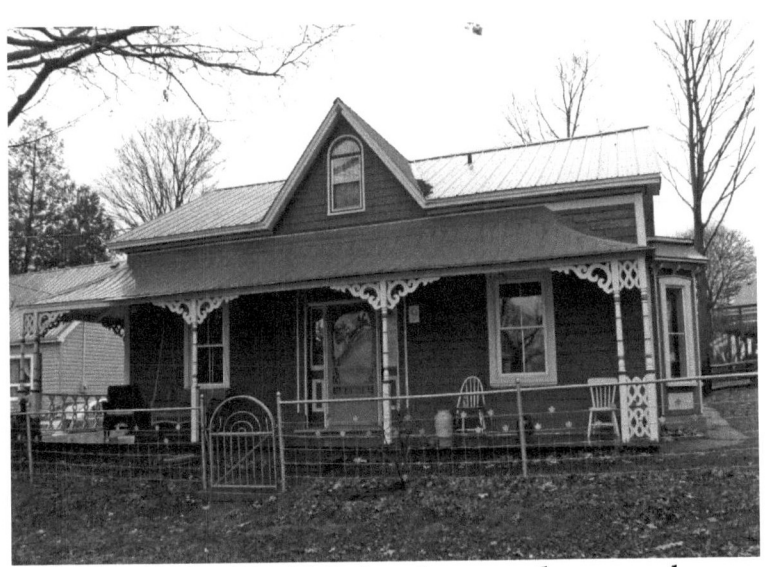

#9 – Regency Cottage with bric-a-brac on the veranda supports

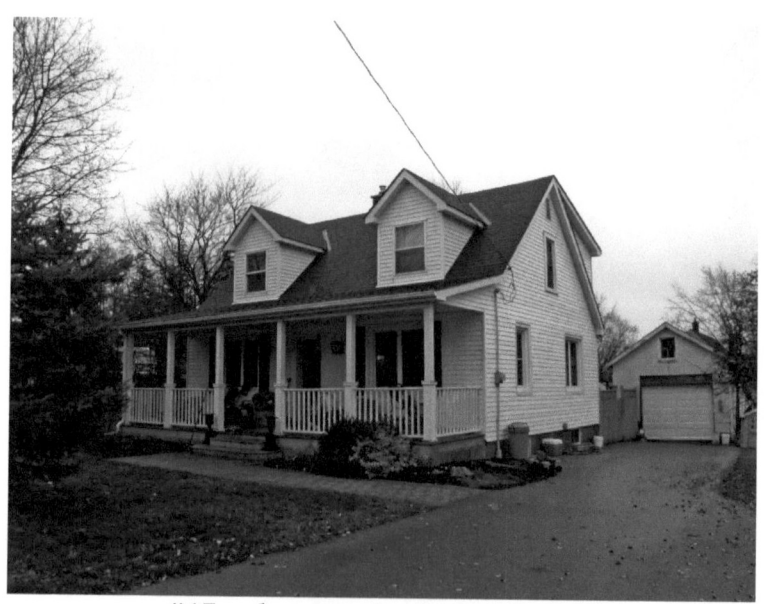

#15 – dormers in the gable roof

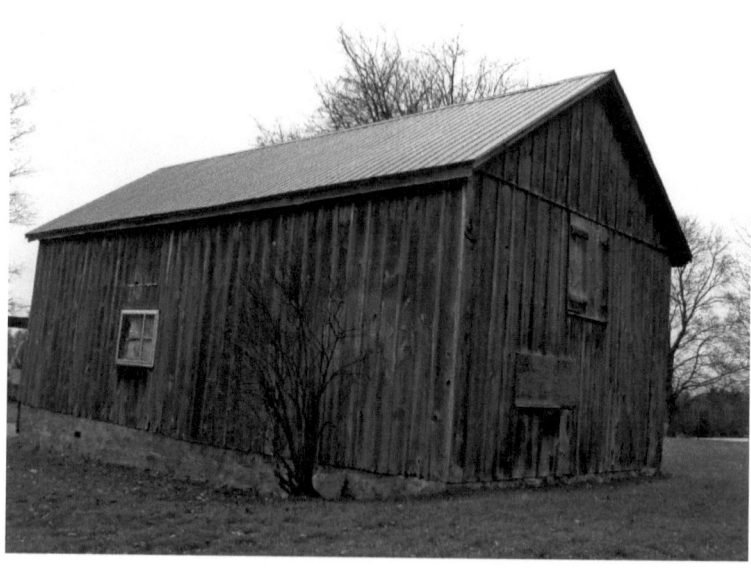

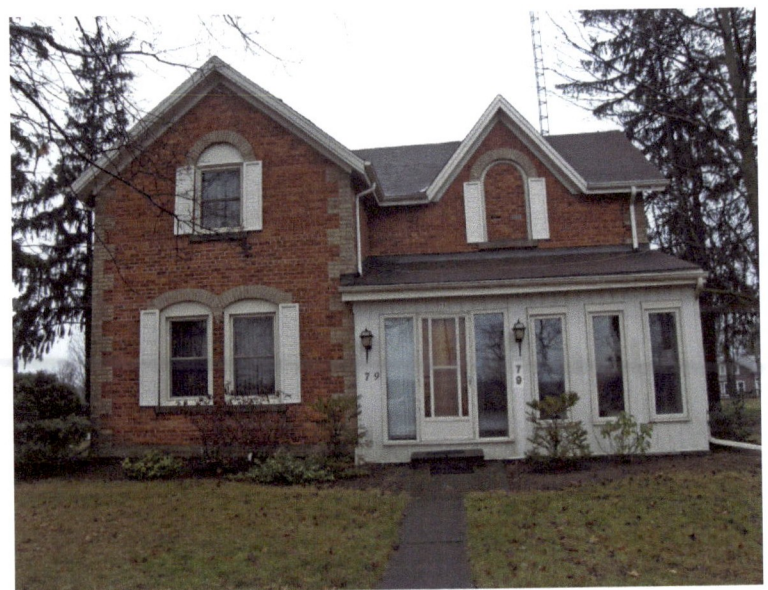

#79 – Gothic – corner quoins

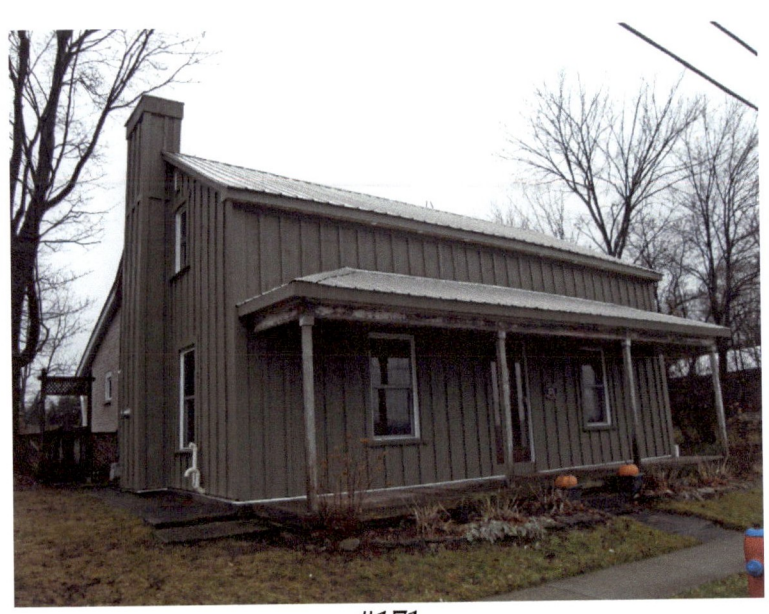

#171

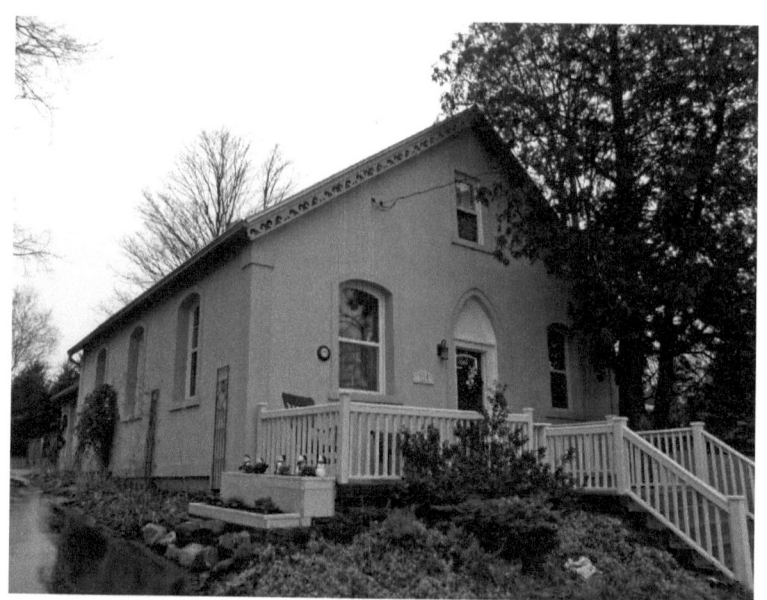

#183

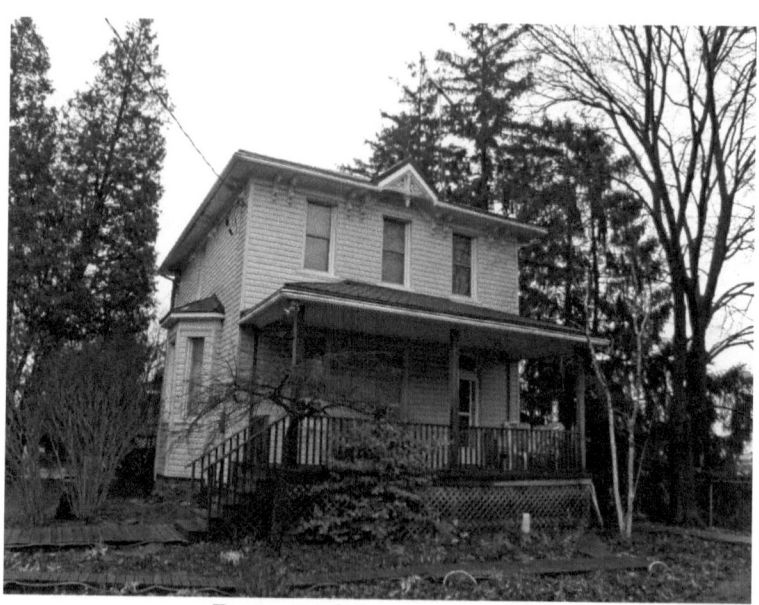

Bay window on the side

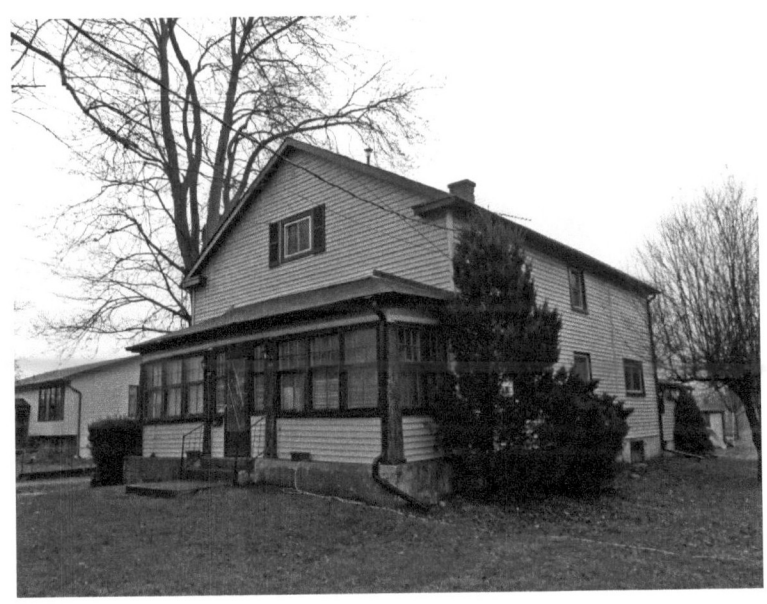

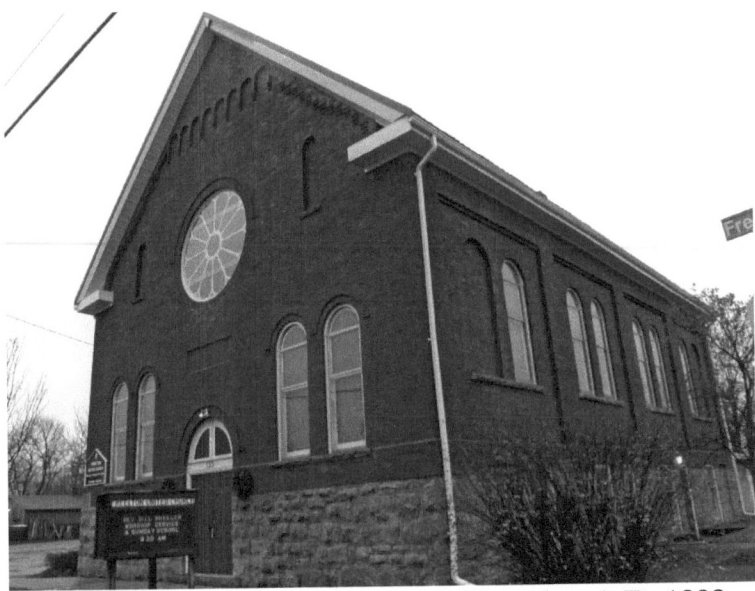

155 Freelton Road – Freelton United Church – A.D. 1899 – rose window, cornice return on gable

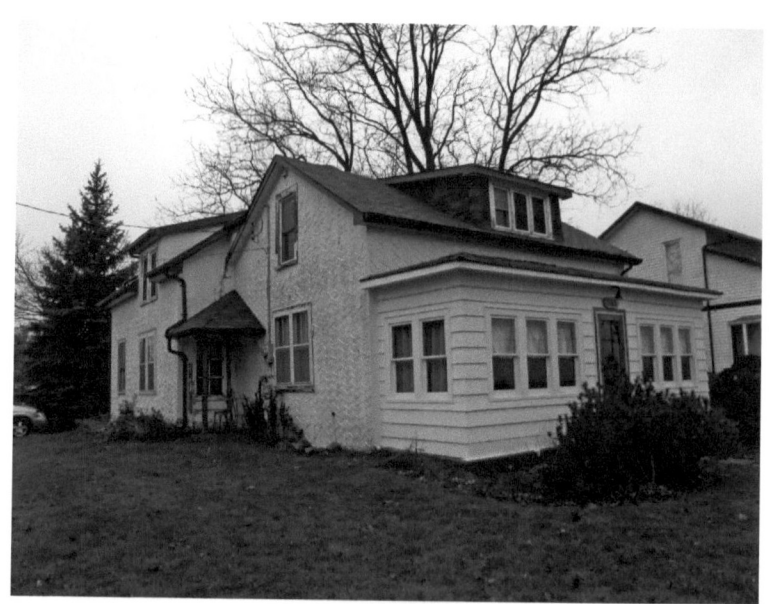

#163

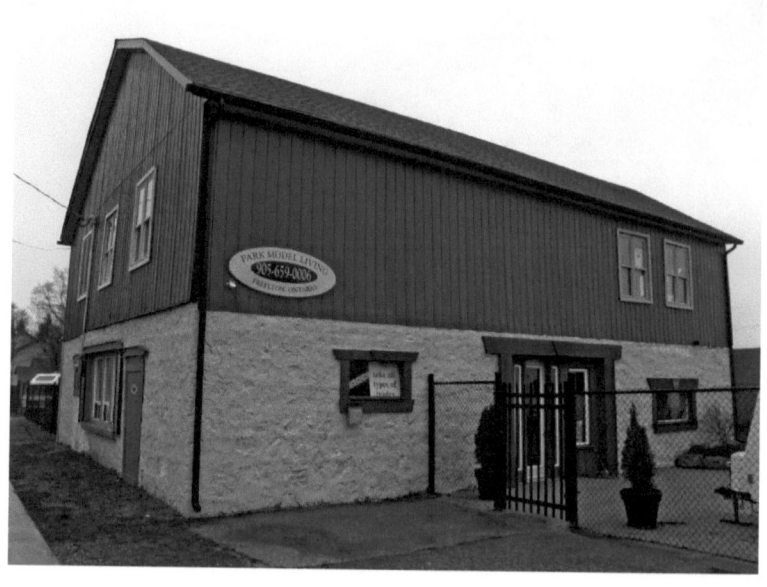

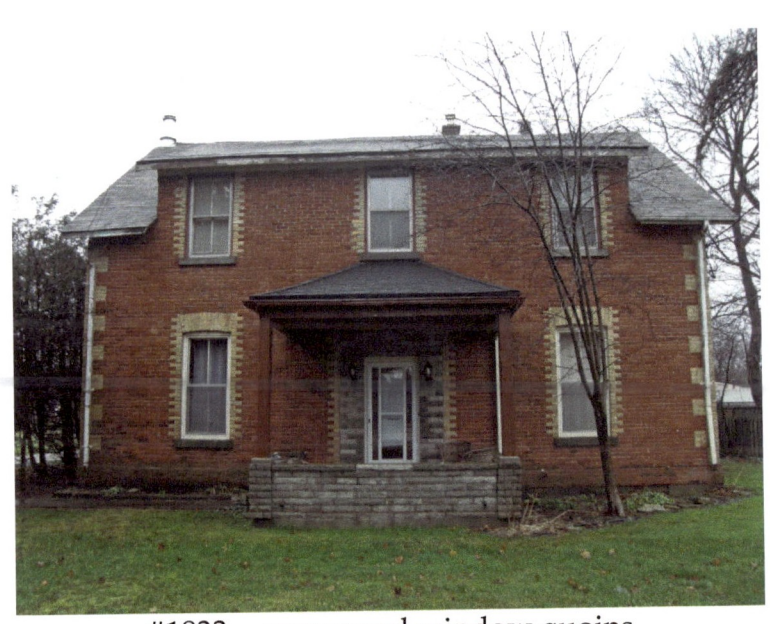

#1833 – corner and window quoins

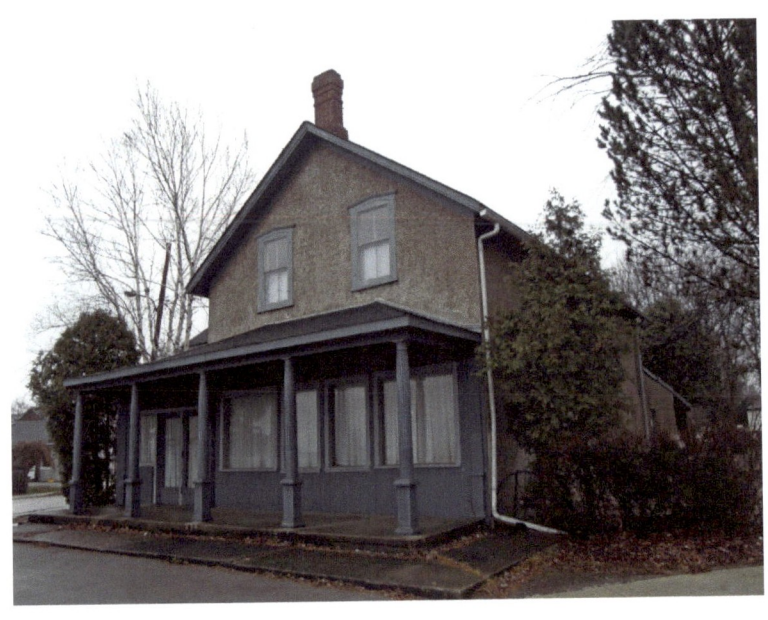

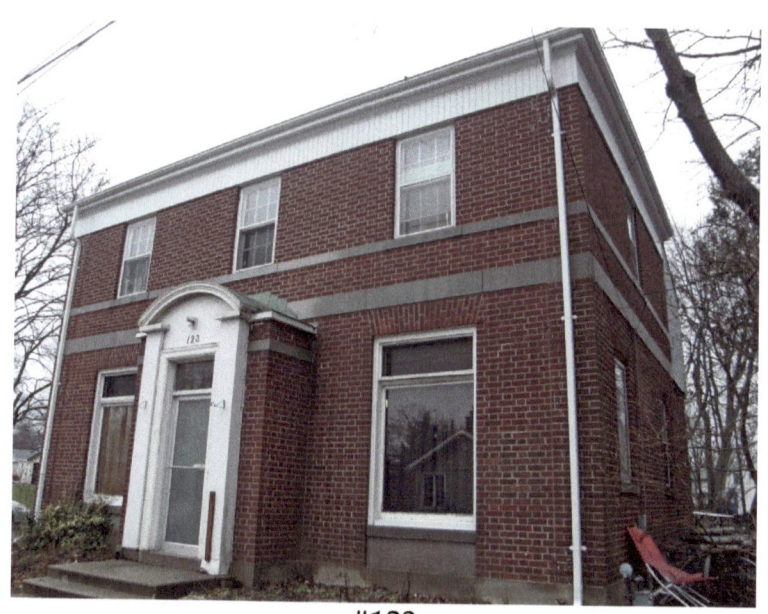

#123

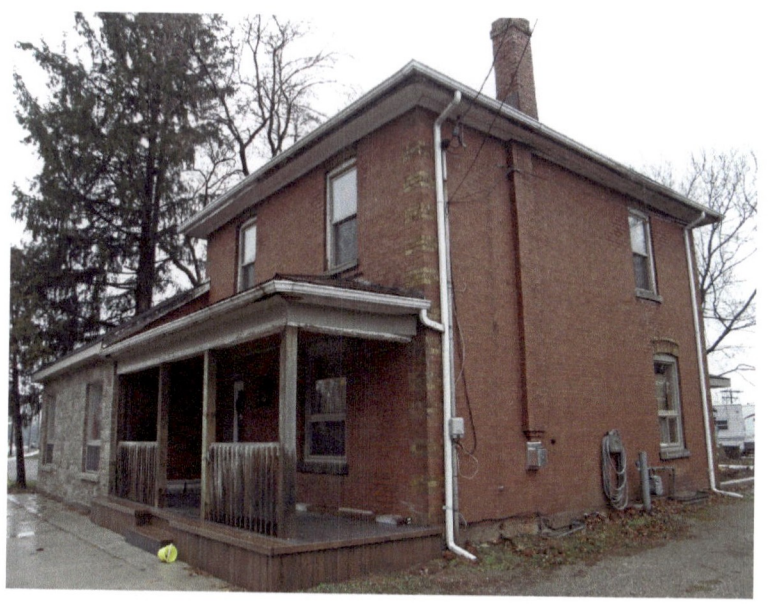

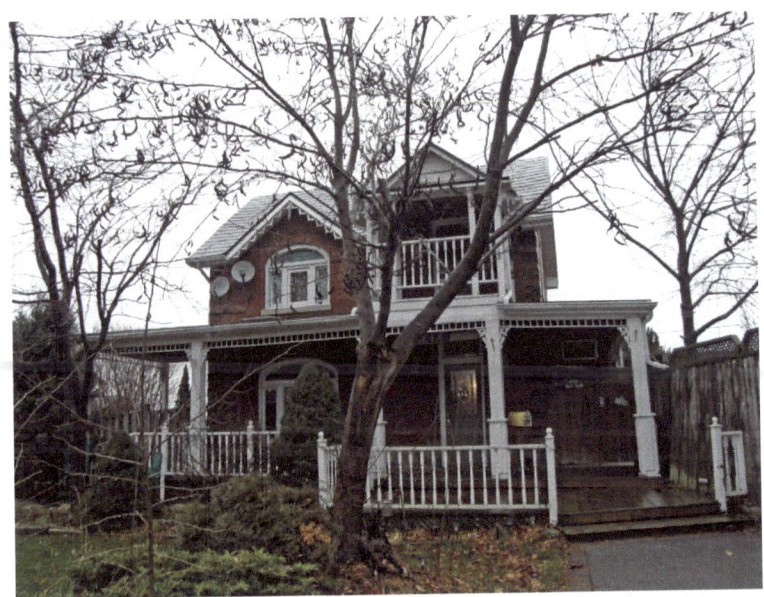

#114 – verge board trim on gable, second floor sleeping porch

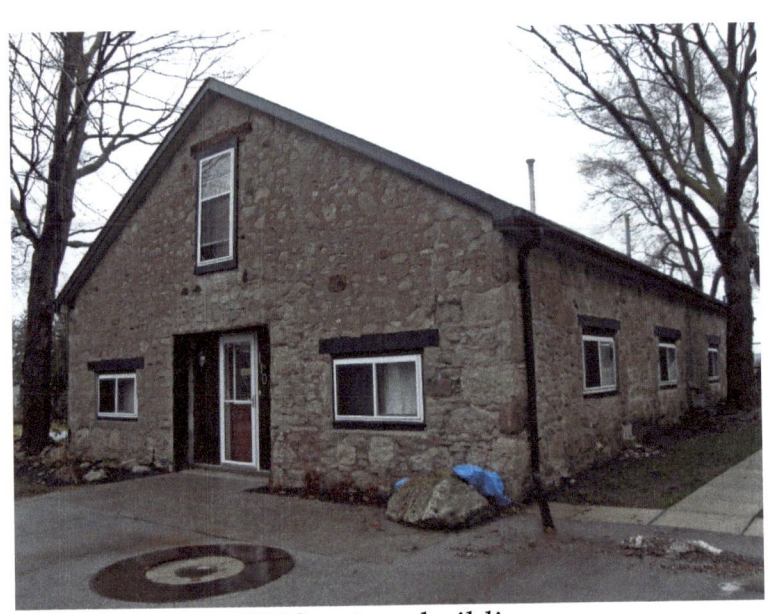

#110 – stone building

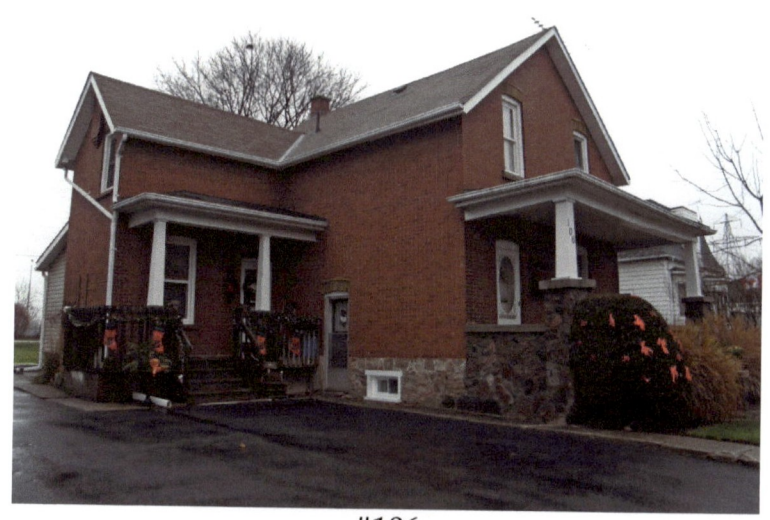

#106

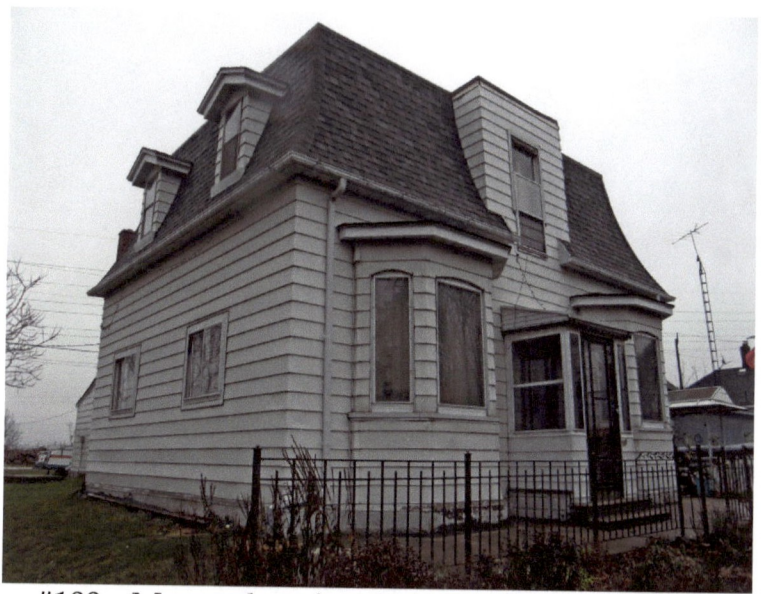

#100 – Mansard roof with dormers, bay windows

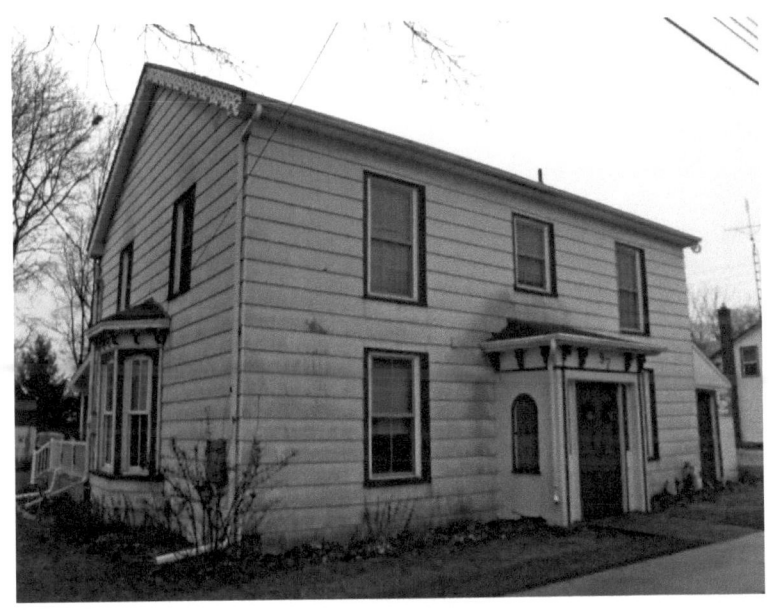

#97 – bay window with brackets, verge board trim on gable

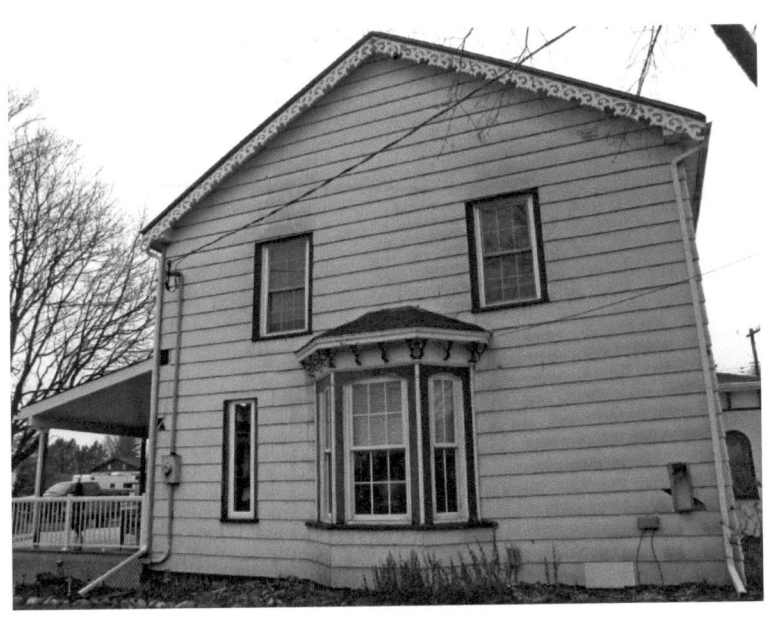

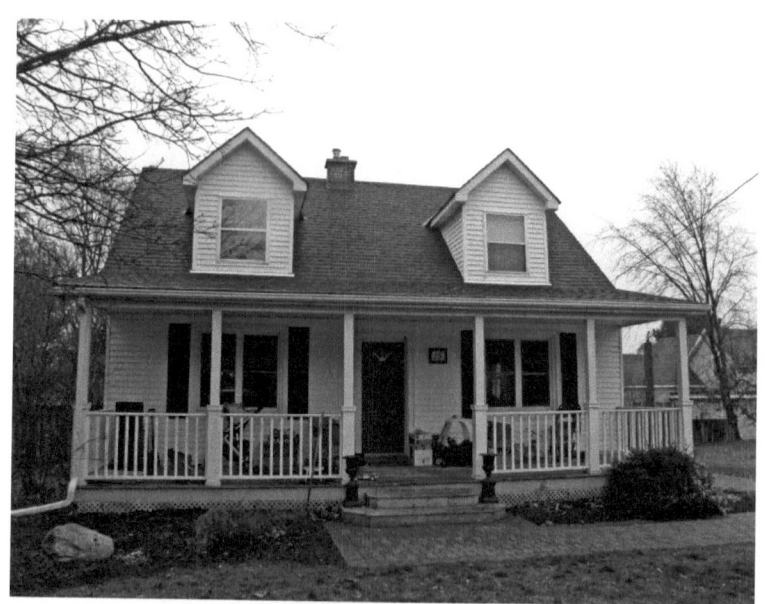

#115 - dormers

Concession 2

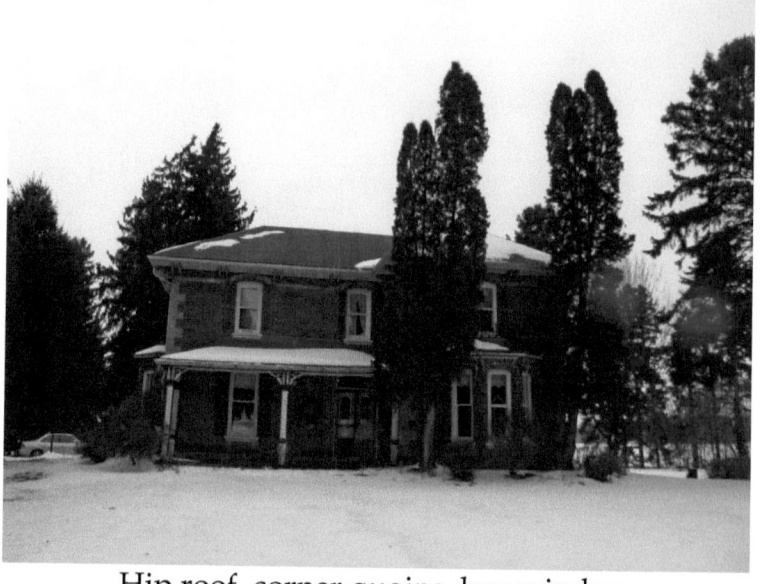

Hip roof, corner quoins, bay window

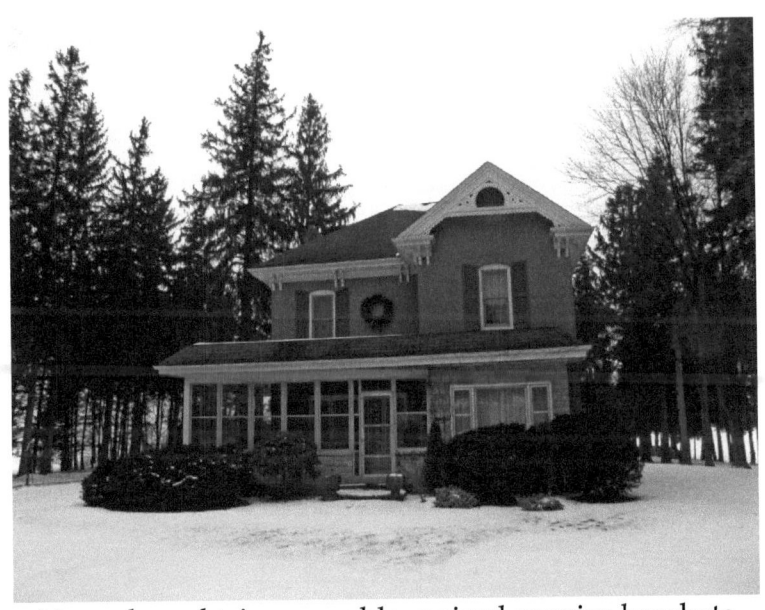

Verge board trim on gable, paired cornice brackets

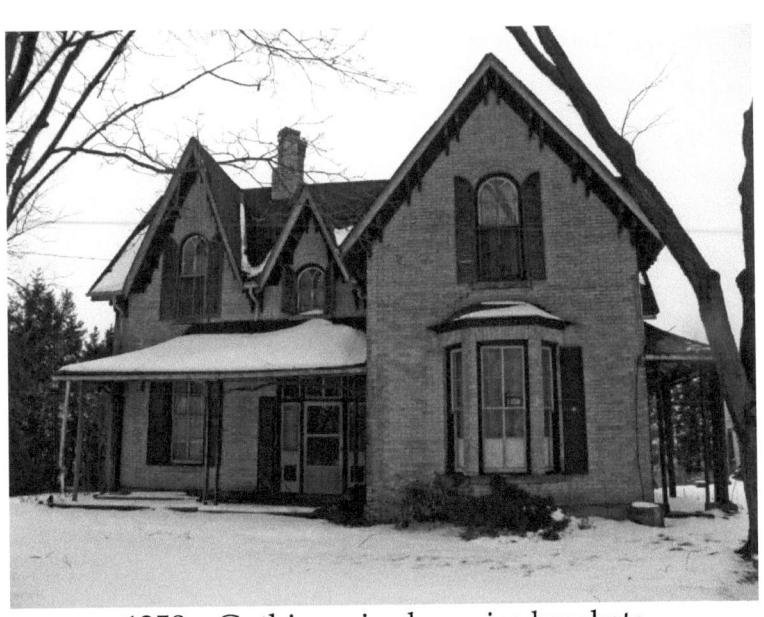

1359 – Gothic, paired cornice brackets

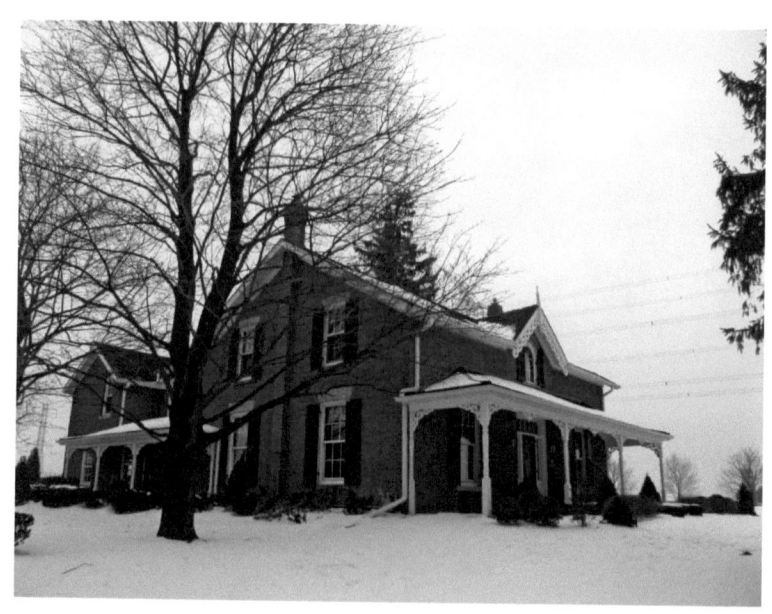

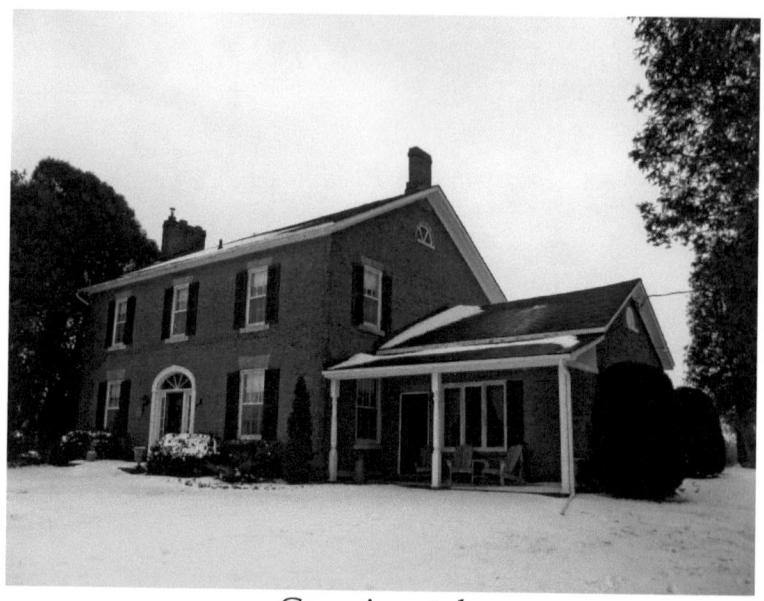

Georgian style

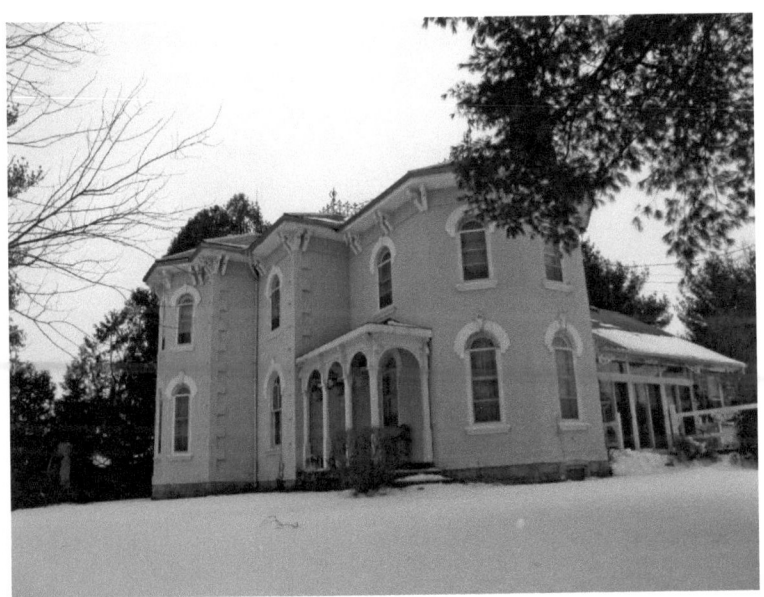

Cornice brackets, corner quoins

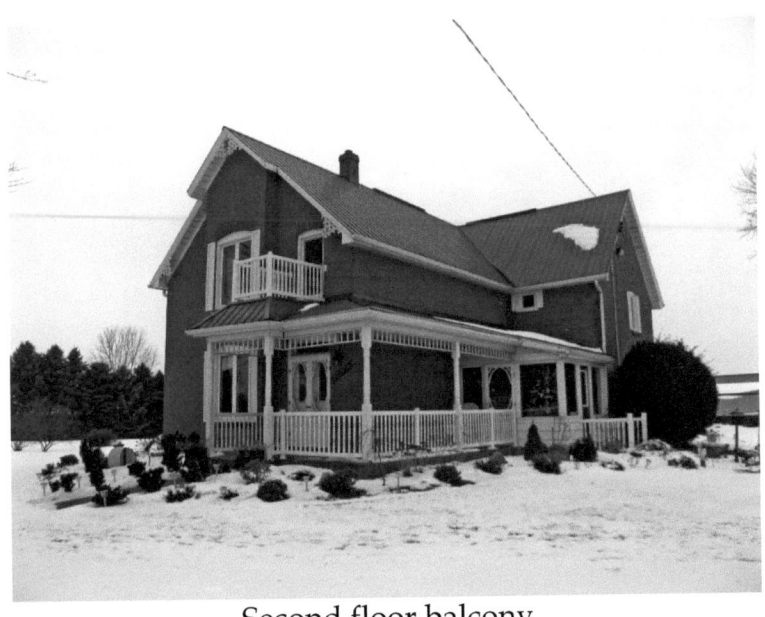

Second floor balcony

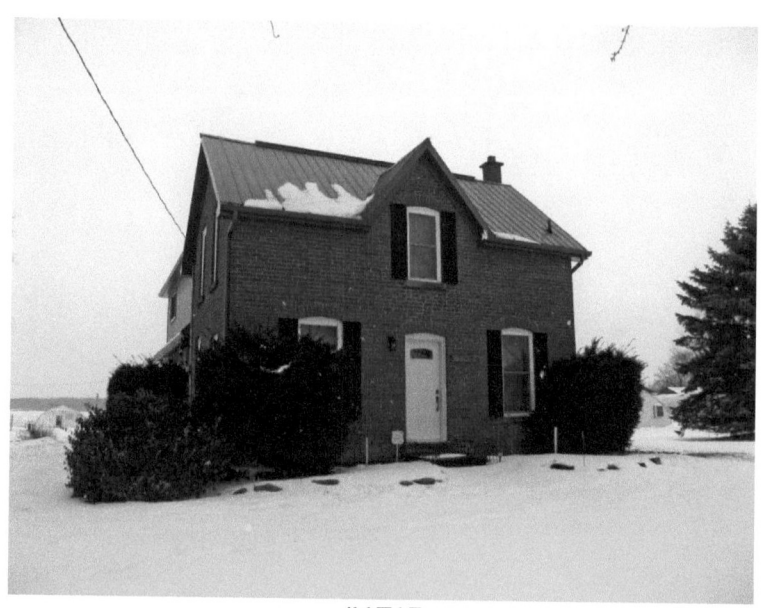

#1715

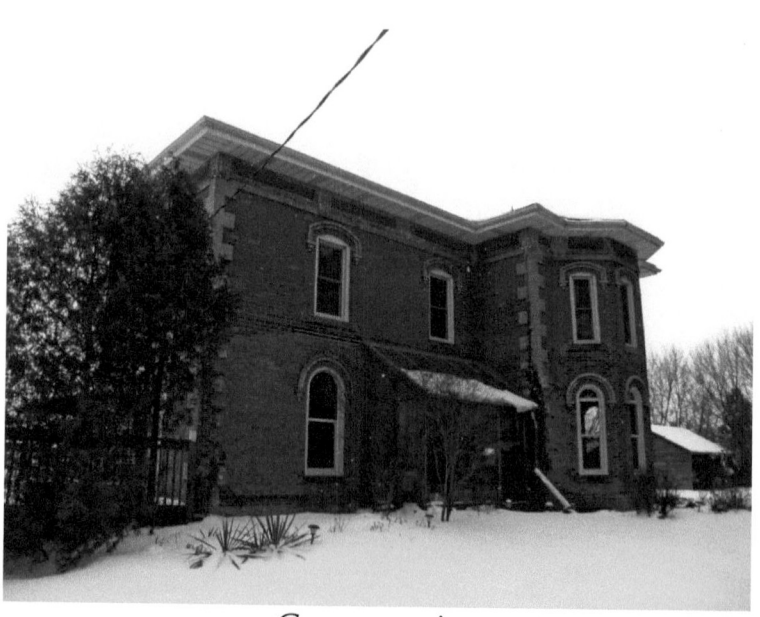

Corner quoins

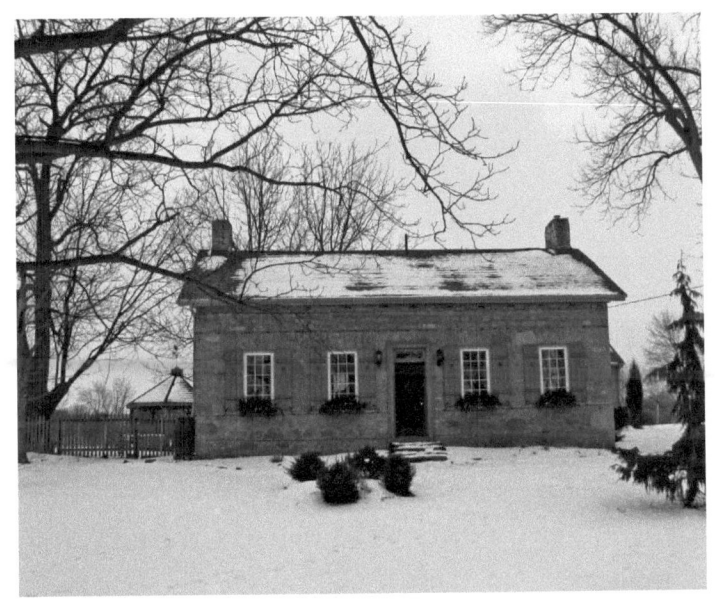

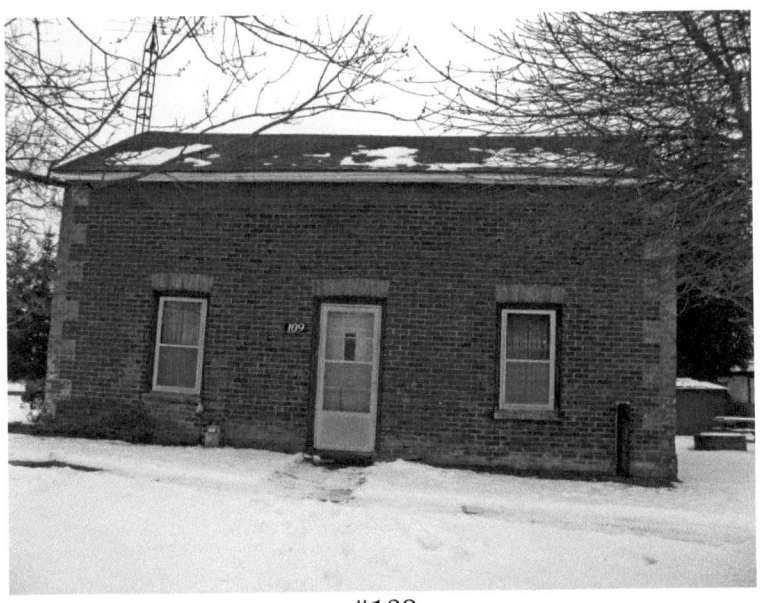

#109

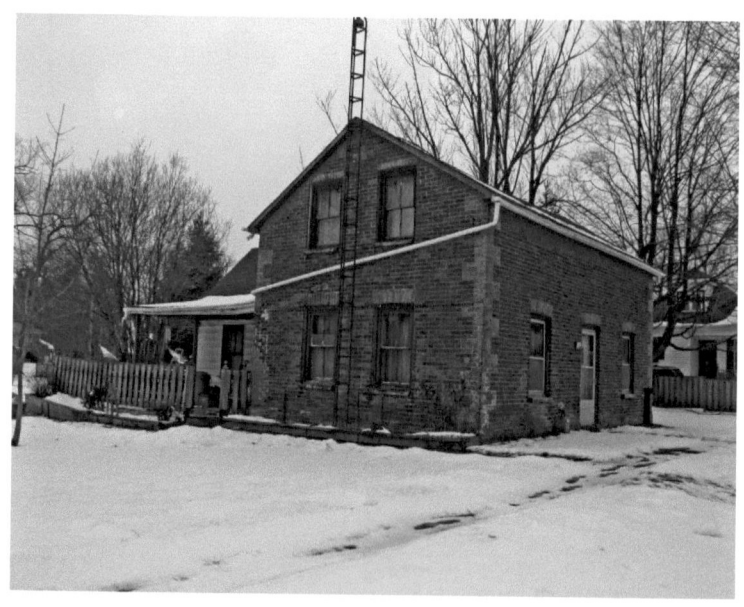

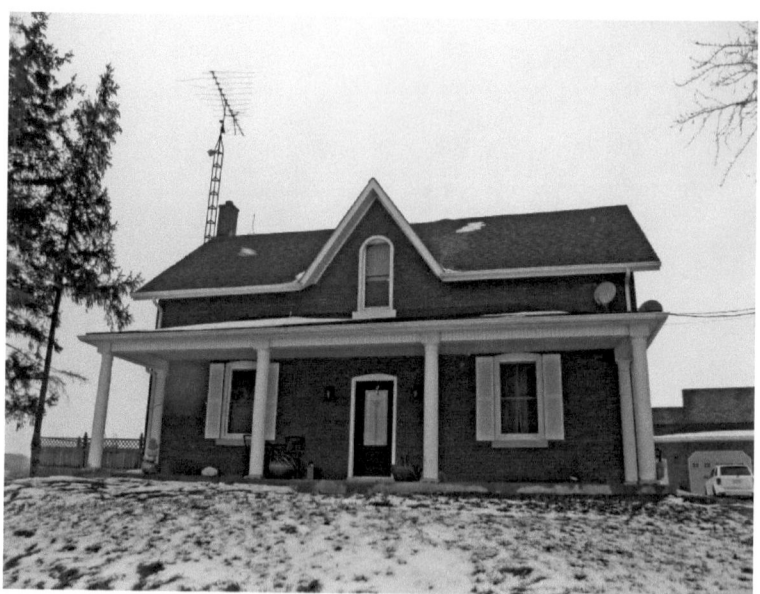

Regency cottage

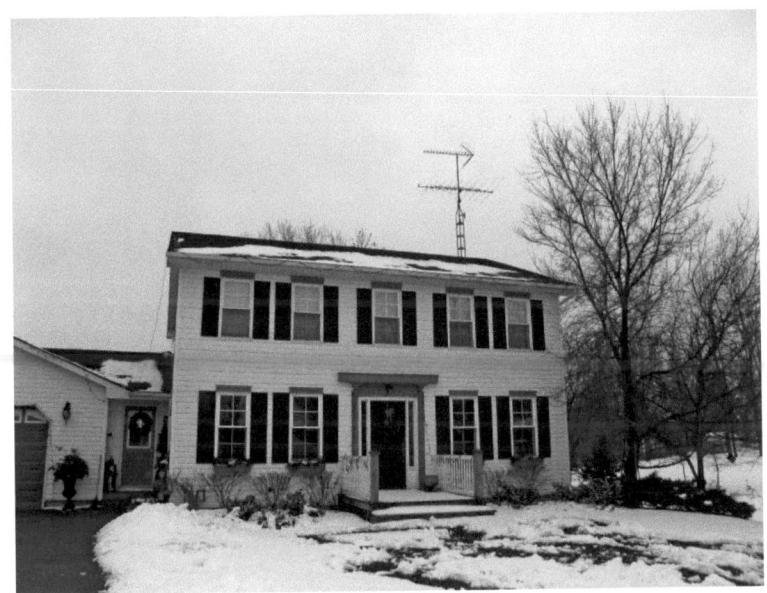

Georgian

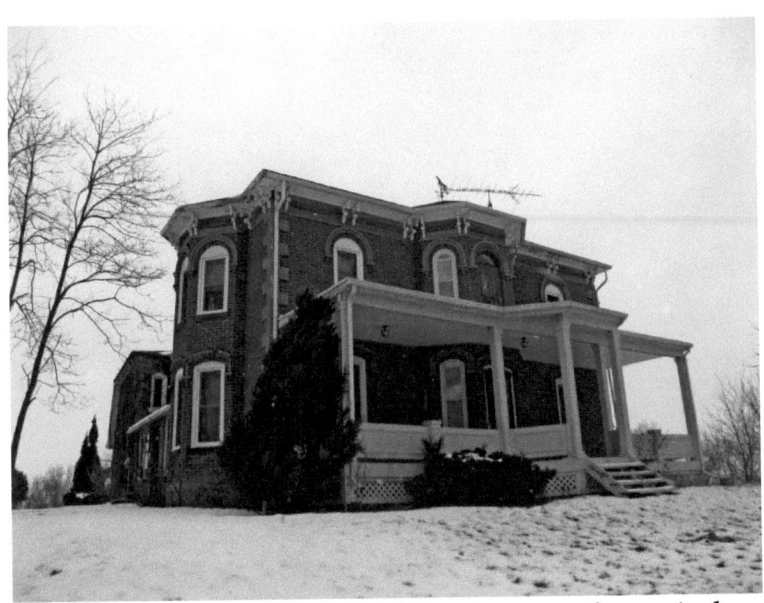

Cornice brackets, corner quoins, two-story bay windows

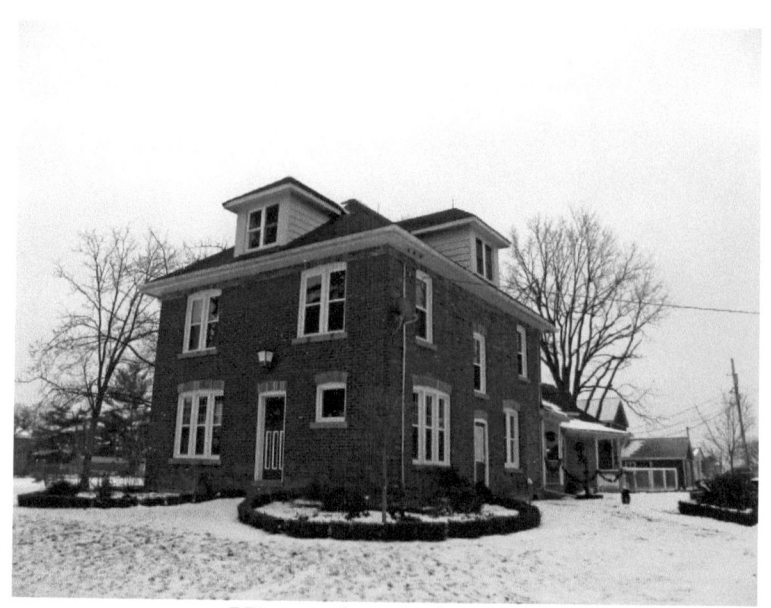
Hip roof with dormers

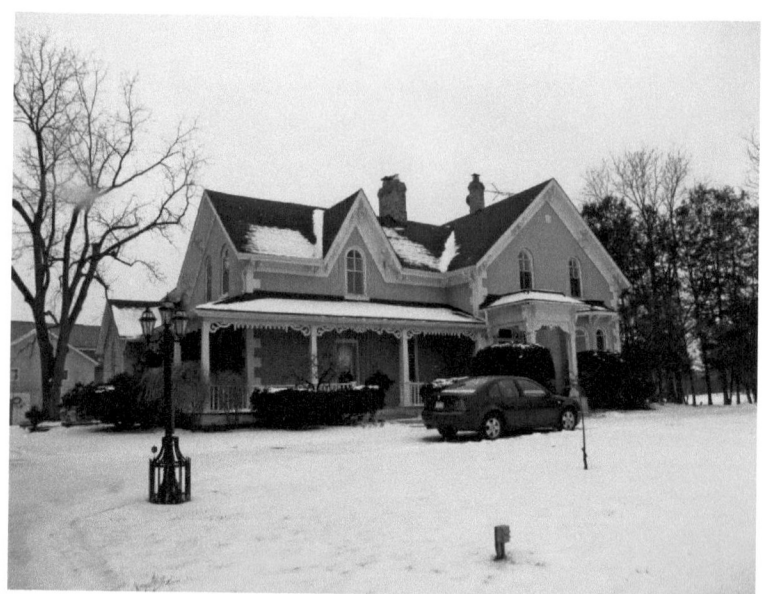
#100 – Fairview – 1878 – Gothic – bric-a-brac on veranda

Concession 4 West

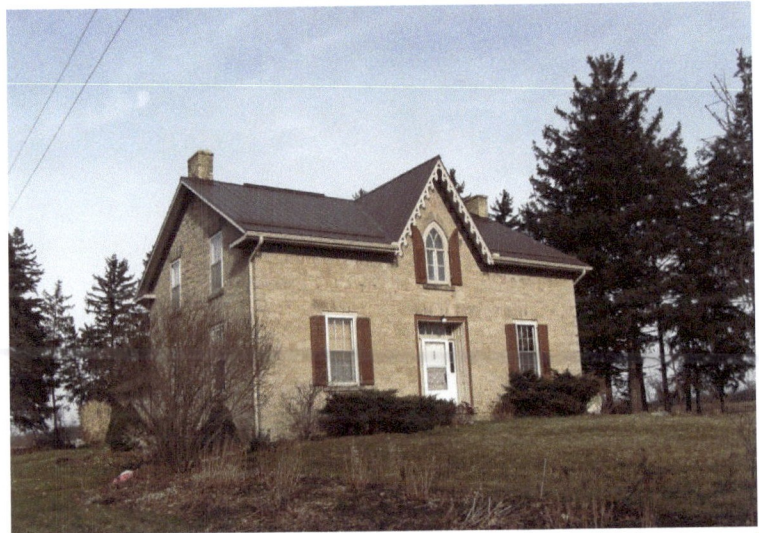

993 Concession 4 West – Gothic – verge board trim on gable

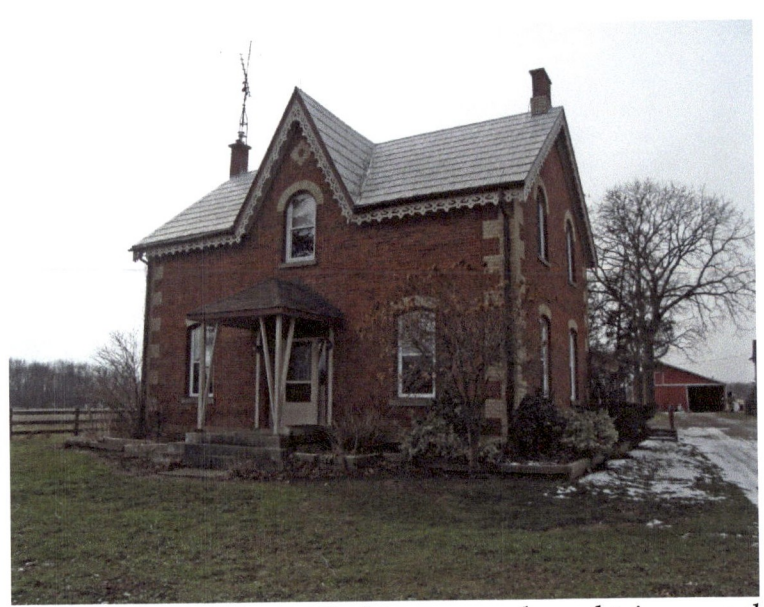

673 Concession 4 West – Gothic – verge board trim on gable, corner quoins

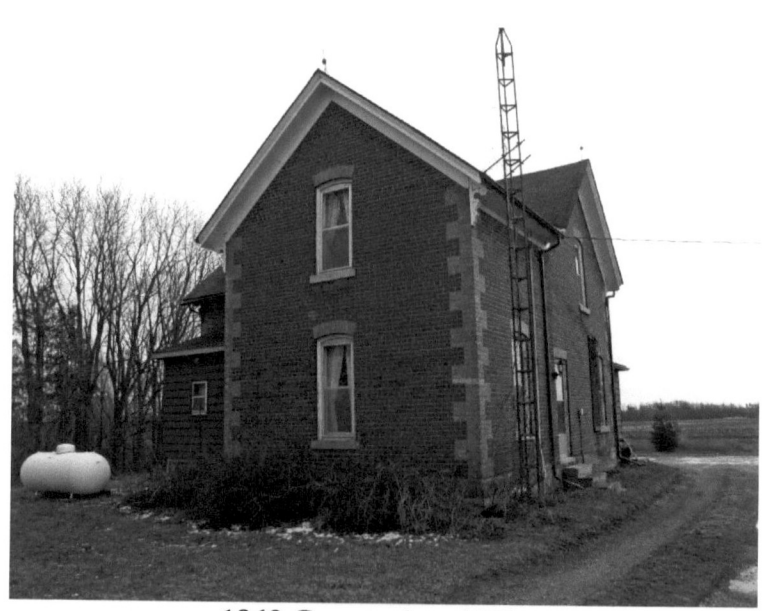

1960 Concession 4 West

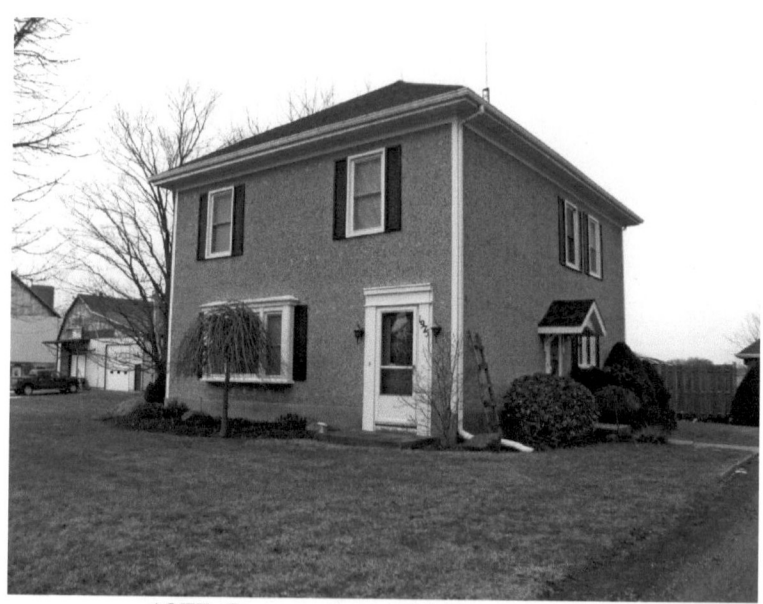

1975 Concession 4 West – hip roof

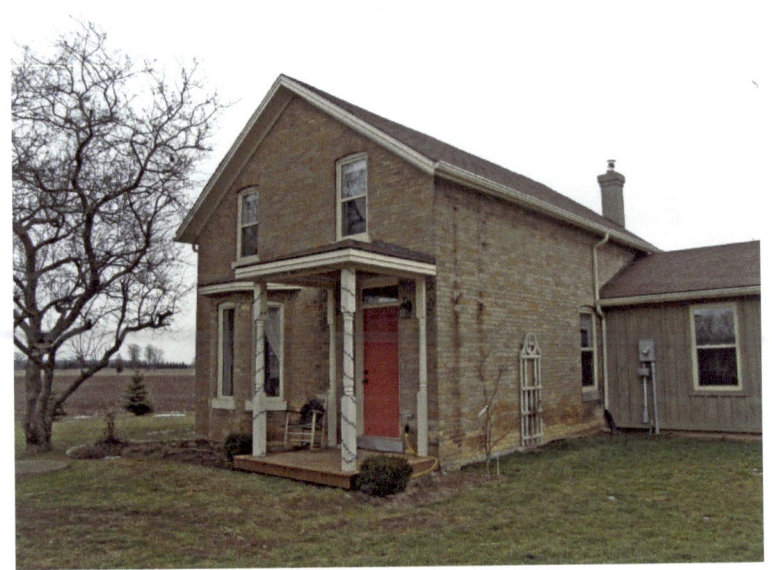

2439 Concession 4 West

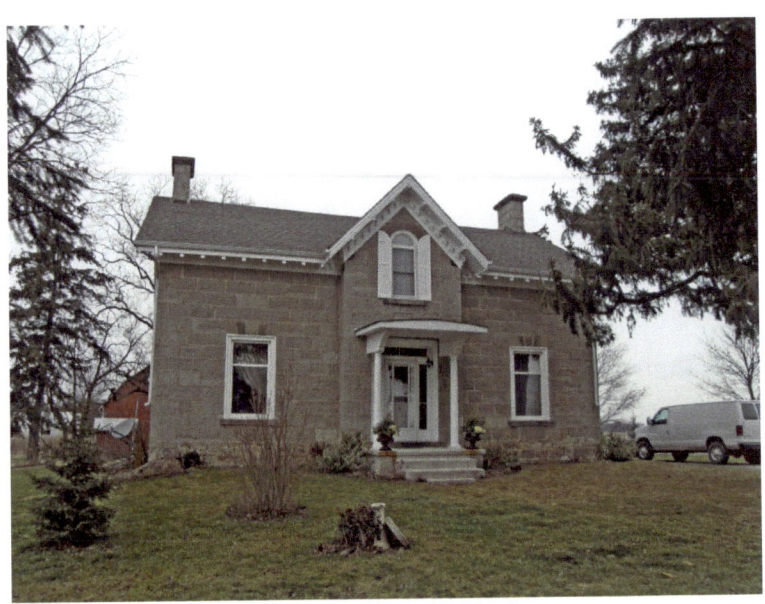

Concession 4 West

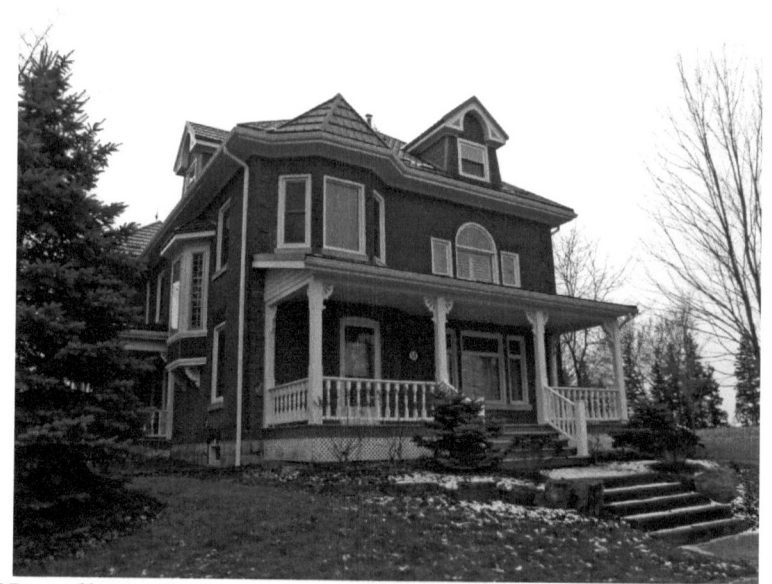

14 Howell Road – dormers, oriel window on left side, two-story bay window on right side, Palladian-type window above veranda

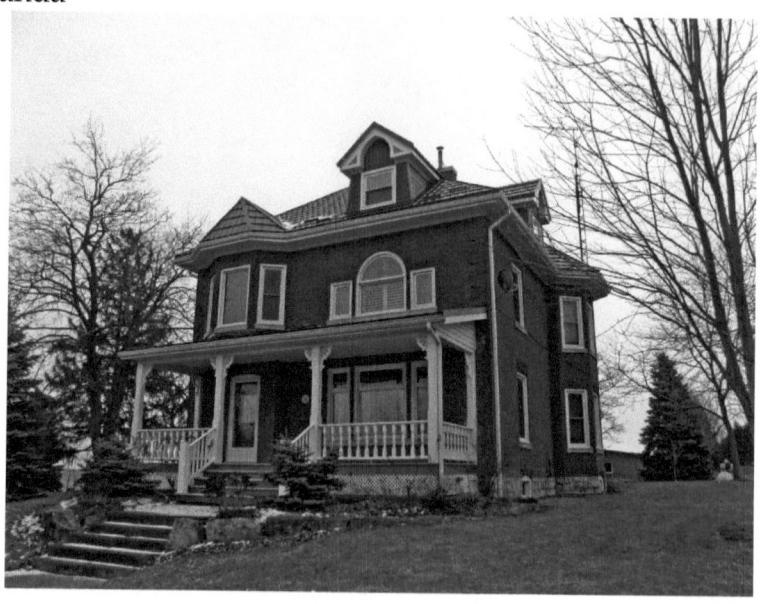

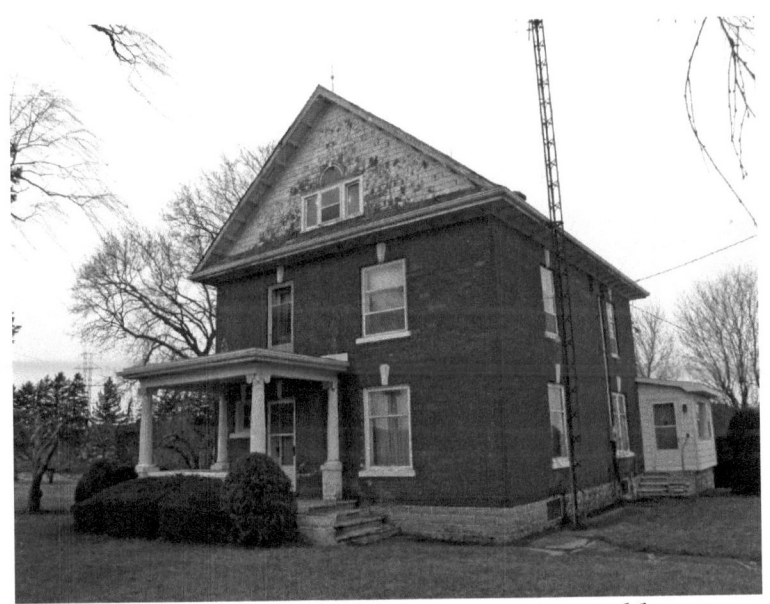

69 Howell Road – Edwardian – voussoirs and keystones

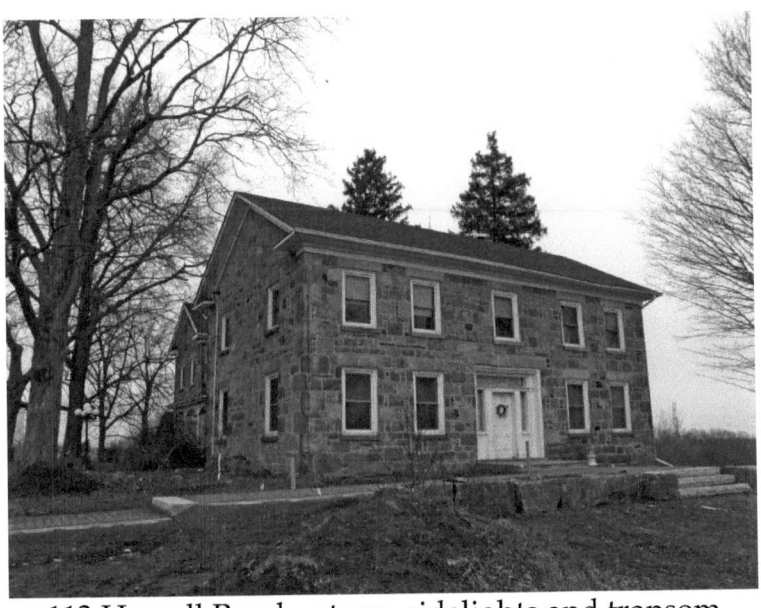

113 Howell Road – stone, sidelights and transom

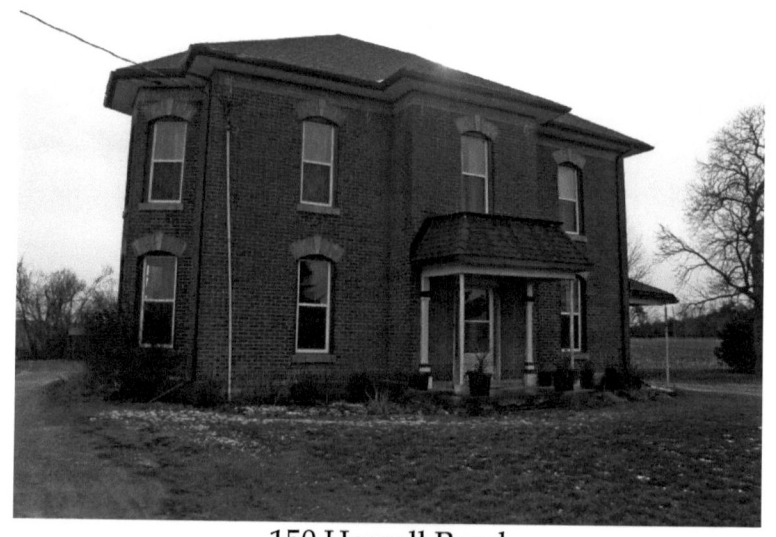

150 Howell Road

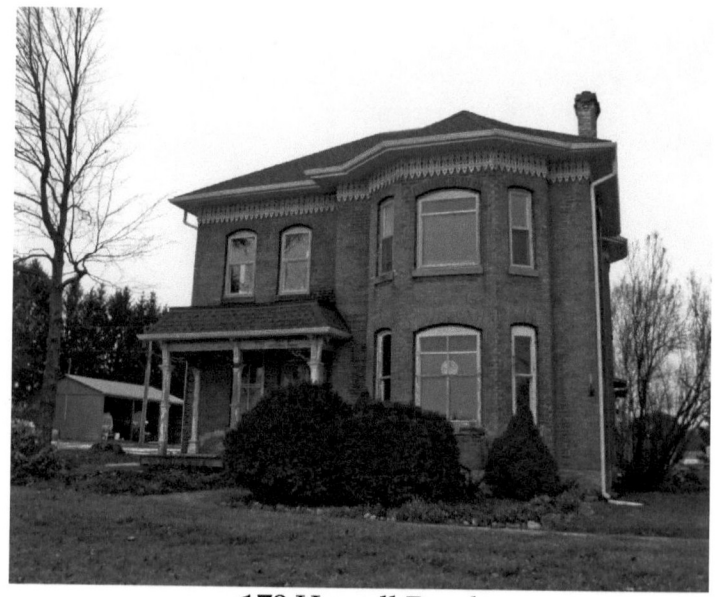

179 Howell Road

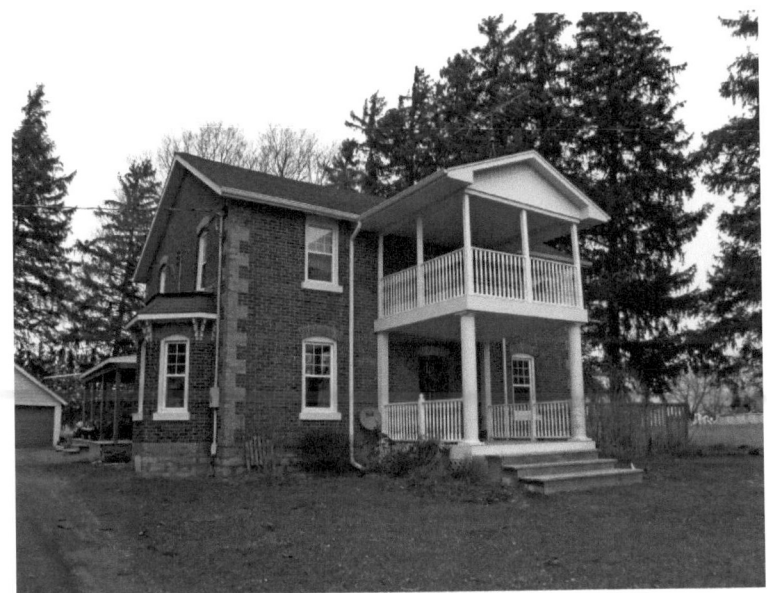

197 Howell Road

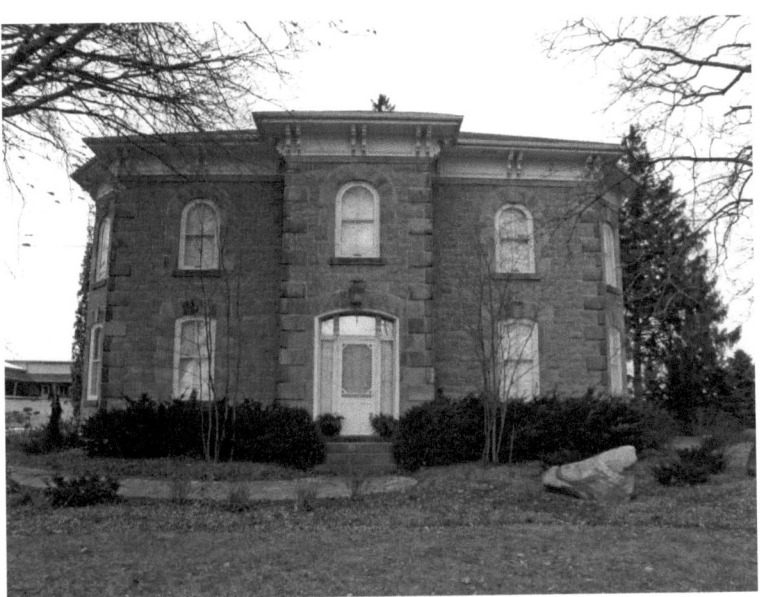

235 Howell Road – Orchard Home Farm – two-story frontispiece with corner quoins, paired cornice brackets

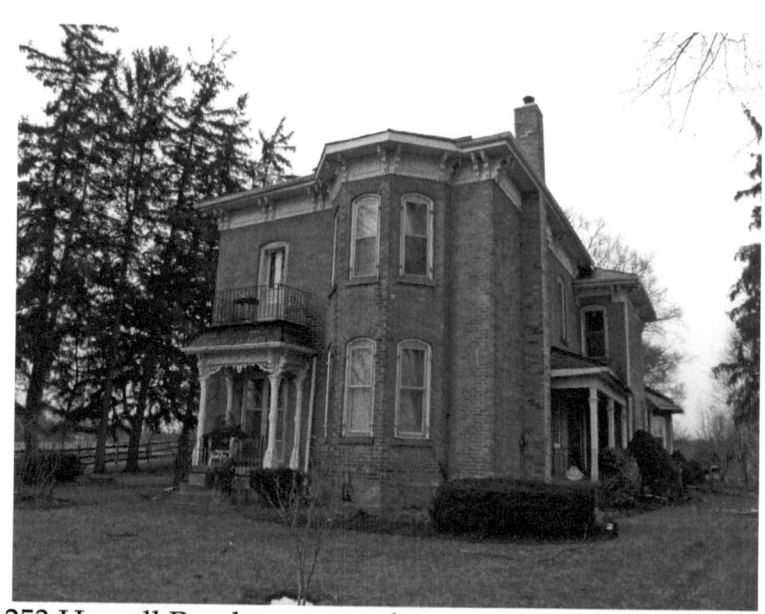
253 Howell Road – century farm – second floor balcony

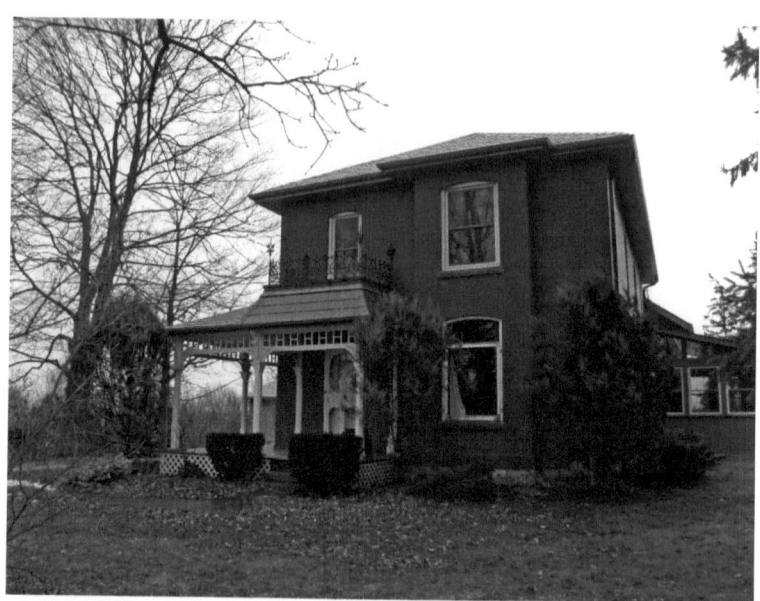
300 Howell Road – iron cresting around balcony

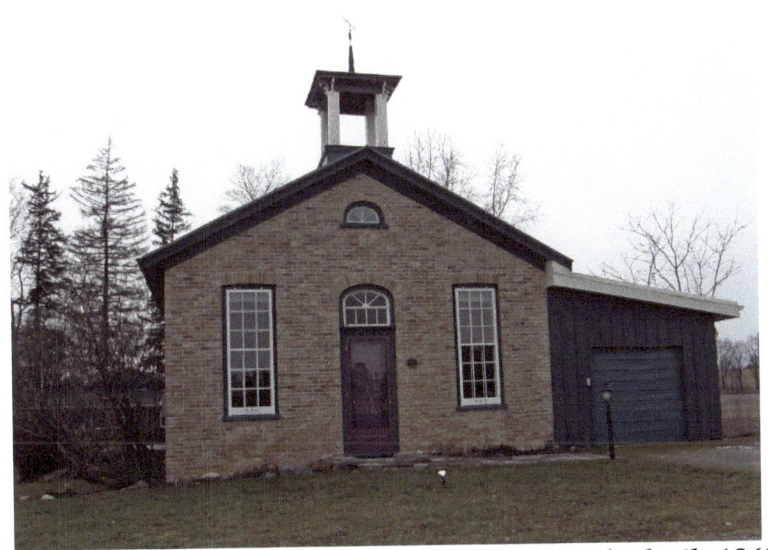

McPherson School Road - McPherson School – built 1869

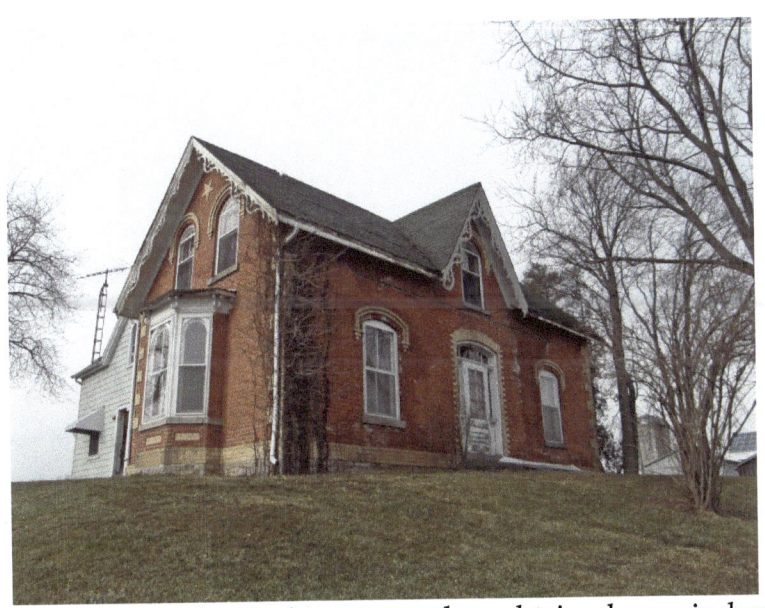

Westover Road – Gothic – verge board trim, bay window

Copetown

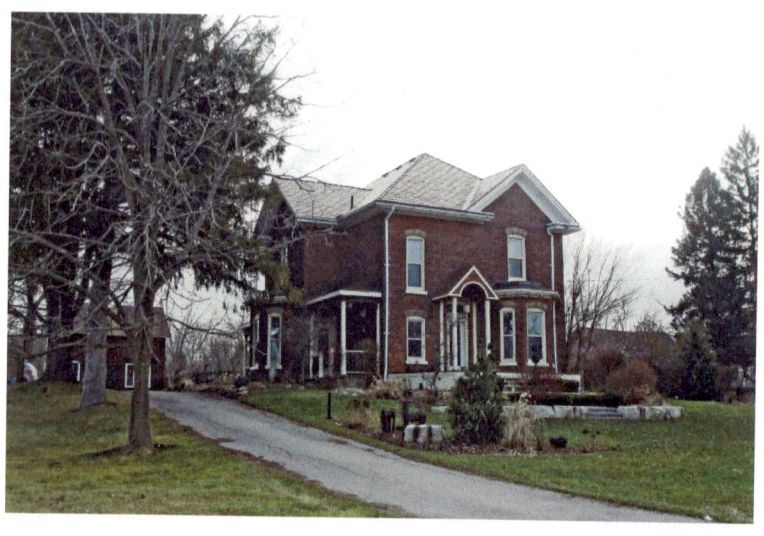

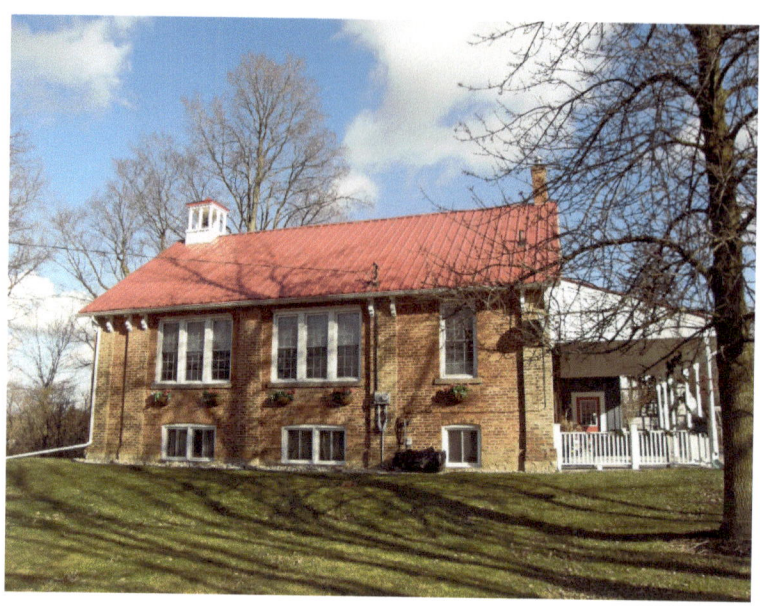

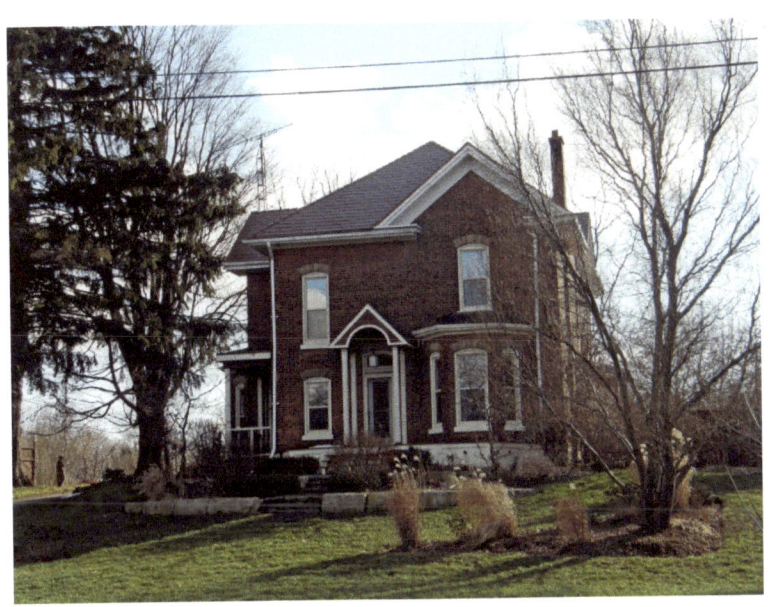

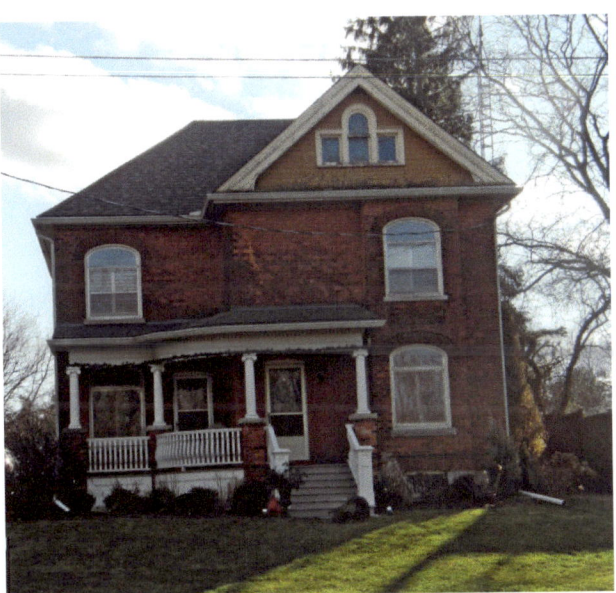

Palladian window in gable

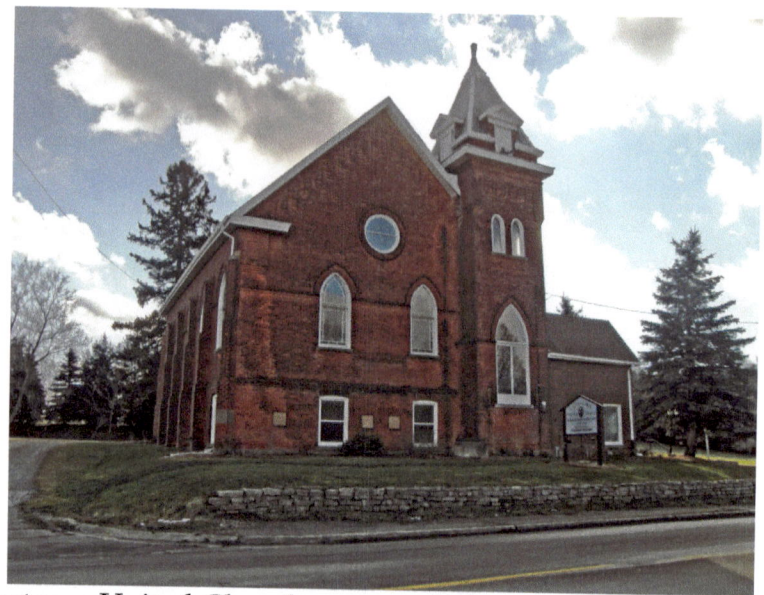

Copetown United Church – rose window, lancet windows, two-story tower

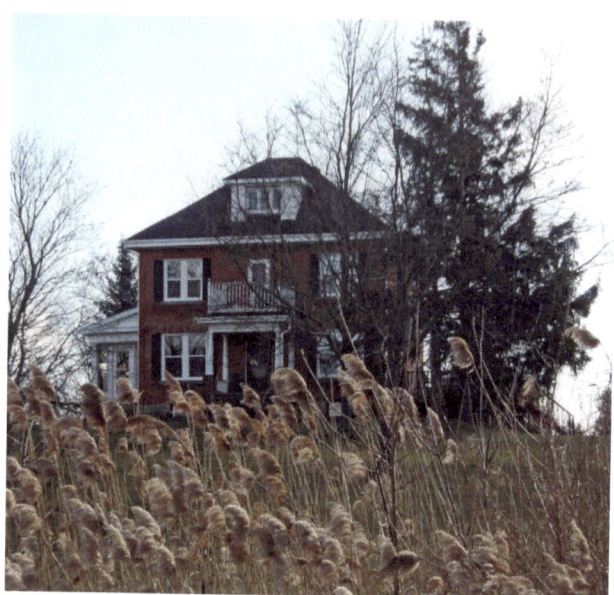

Hip roof with dormer

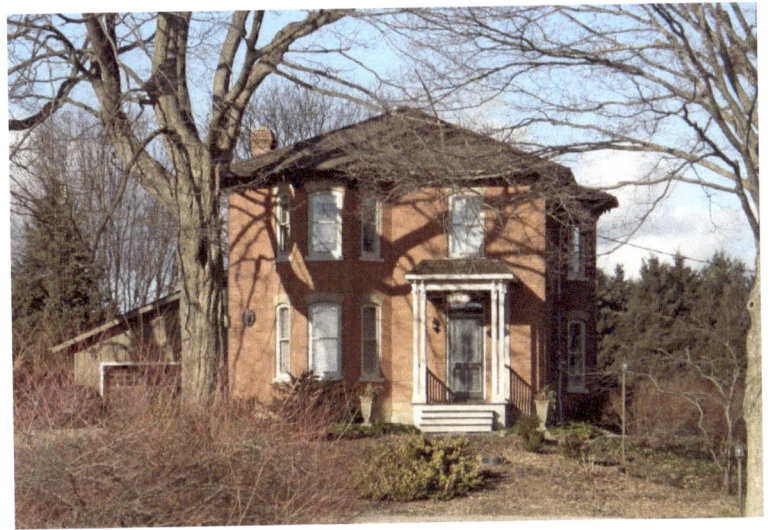

Hip roof

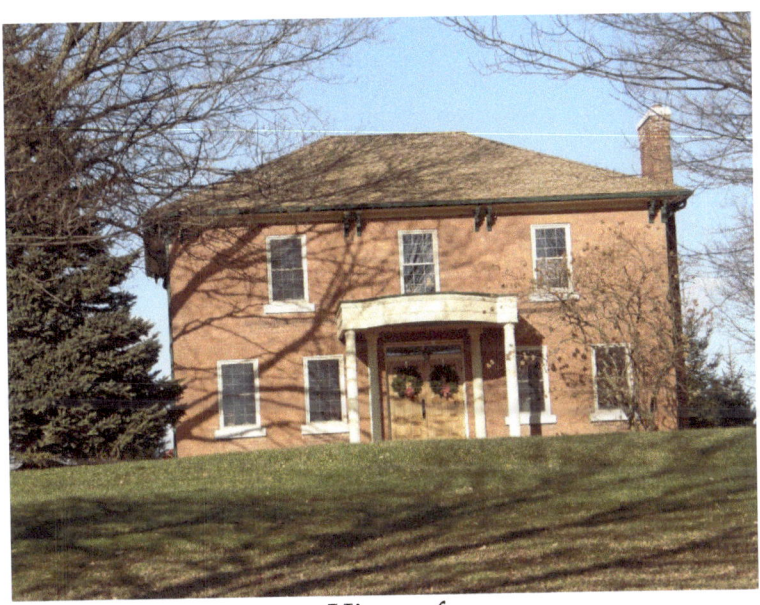

Hip roof

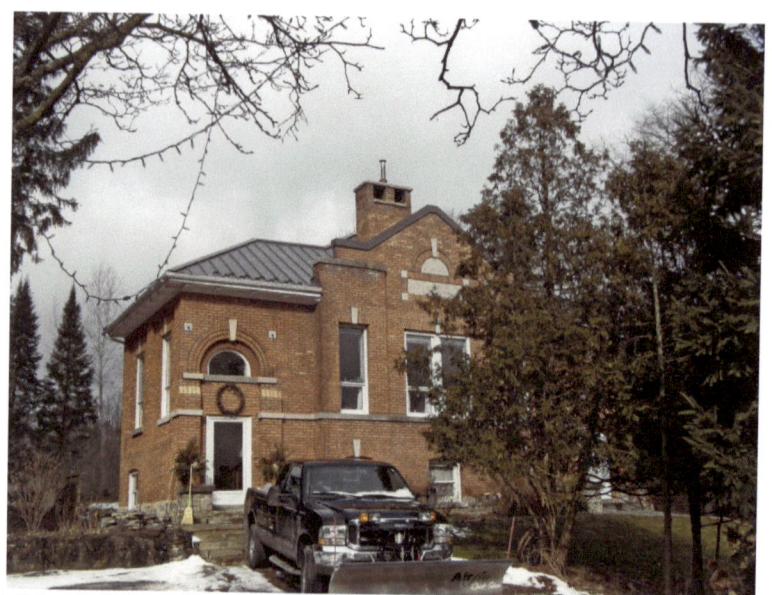

S.S. No. 3 School – West Flamborough and Ancaster – 1916 – voussoirs and keystones

Crieff

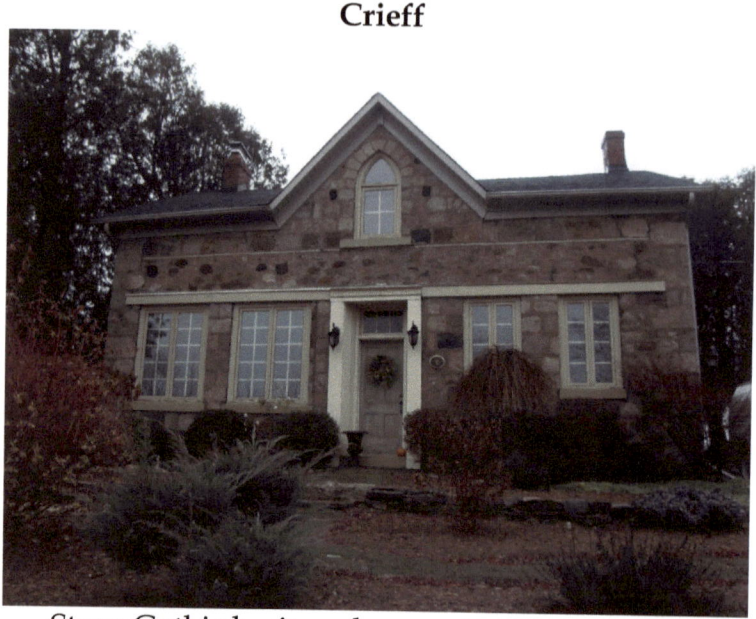

Stone Gothic heritage home – transom window

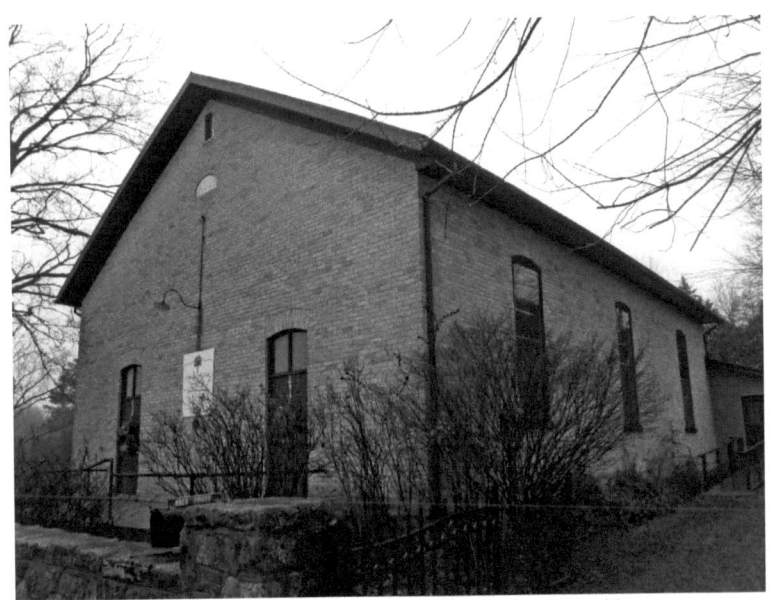
Knox Presbyterian Church Crieff

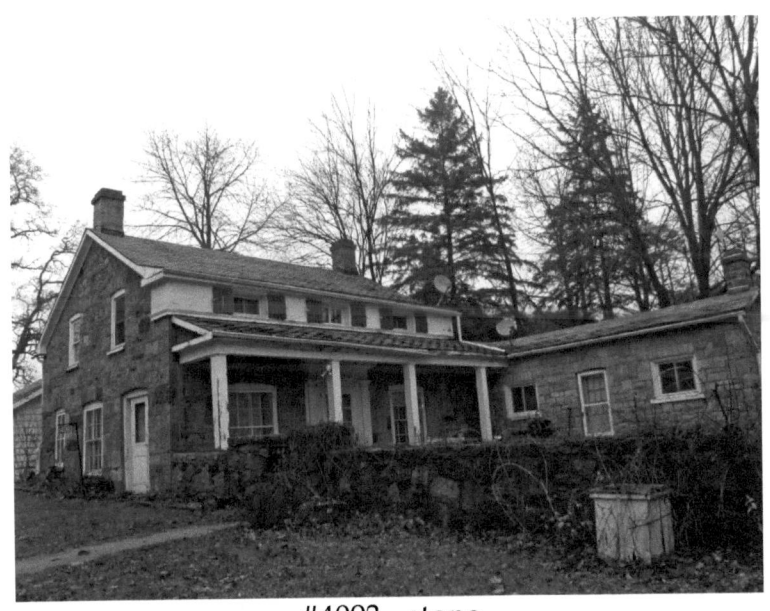
#4093 - stone

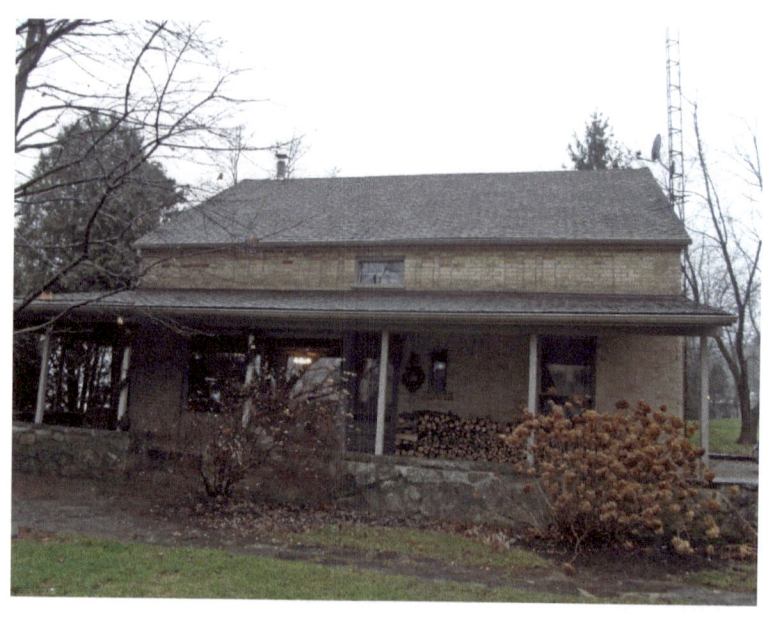

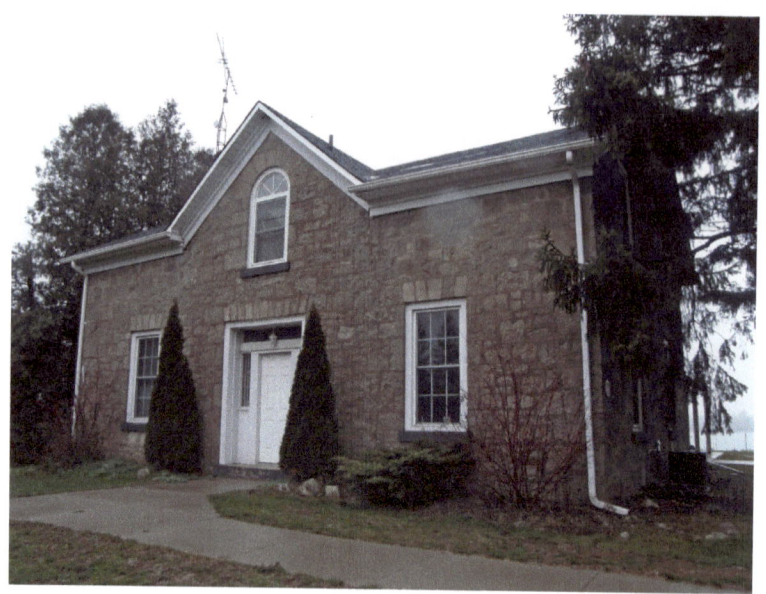

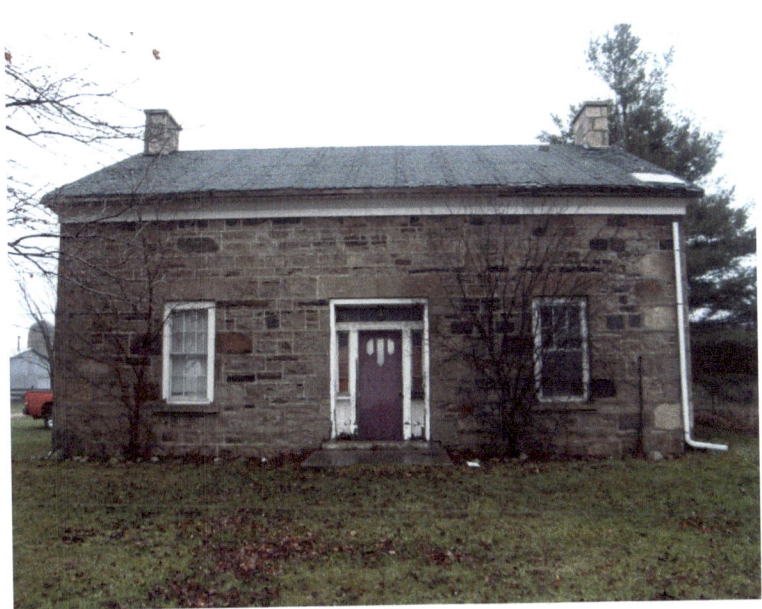

Stone – sidelights and transom

Jerseyville

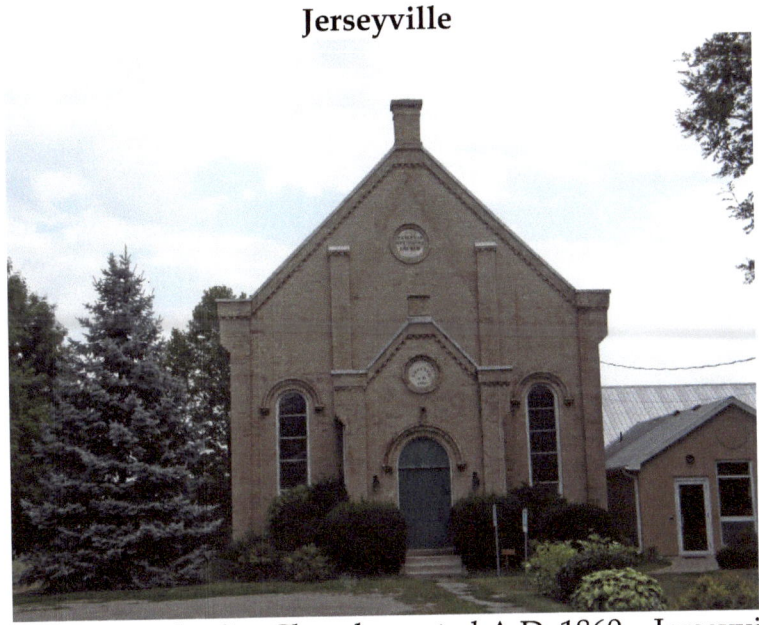

Wesleyan Methodist Church erected A.D. 1860 – Jerseyville

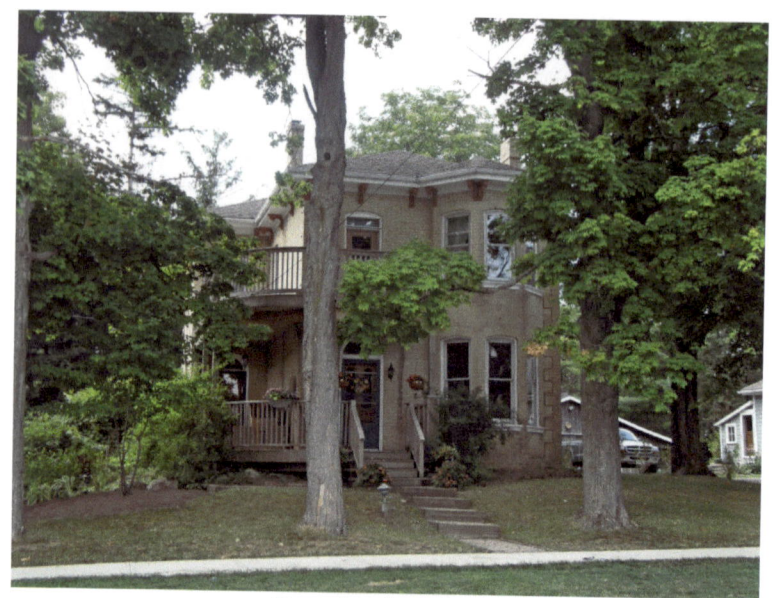

Cornice brackets

Lynden

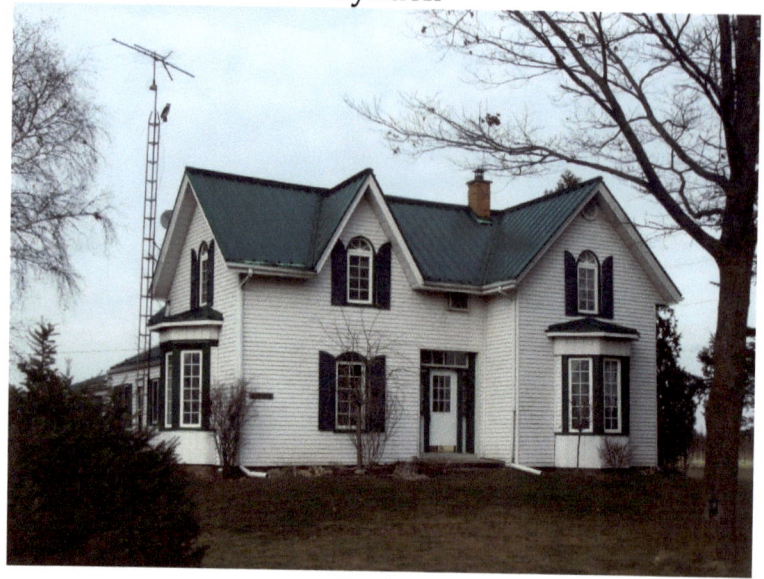

Gothic

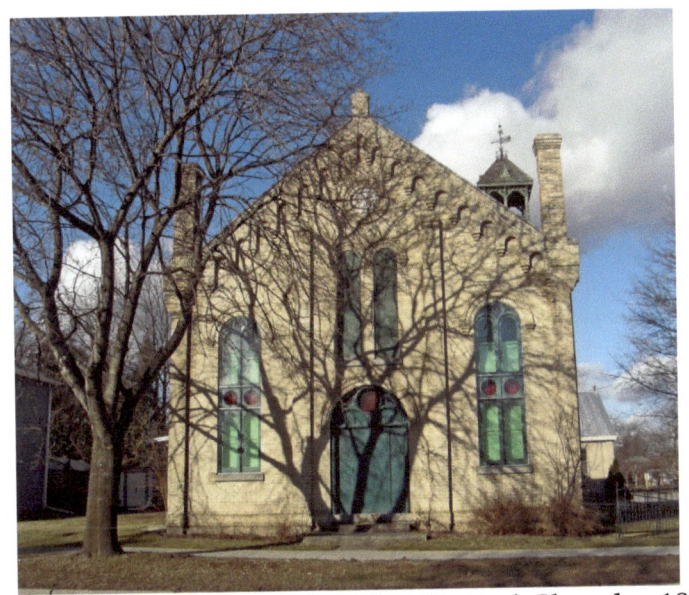

3989 Governor's Road - Lynden United Church - 1870

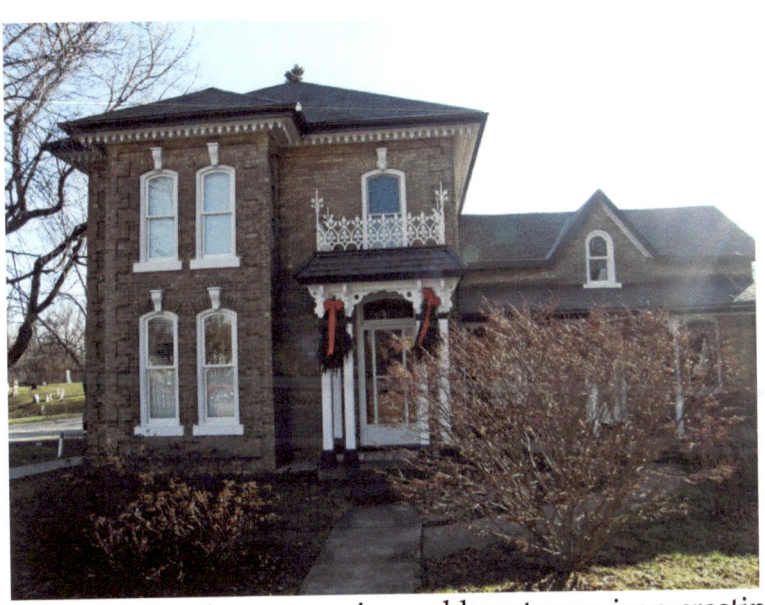

Decorative cornice, voussoirs and keystones, iron cresting above porch, corner quoins

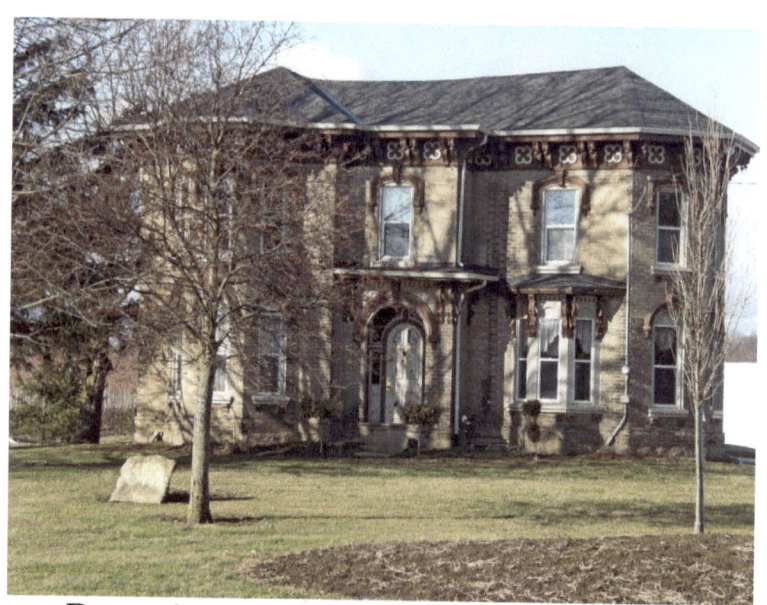
Decorative cornice and brackets, bay window

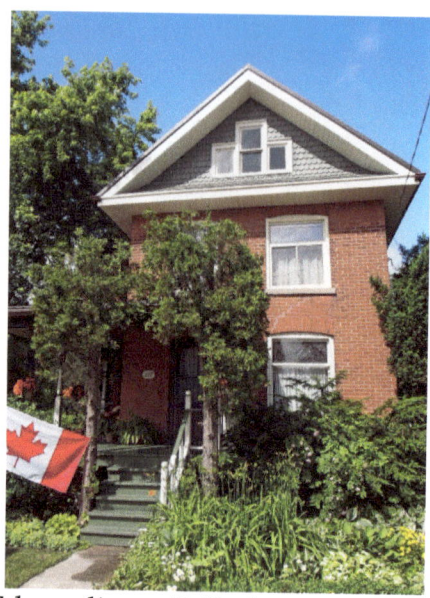
#117 – Edwardian – Palladian window in gable

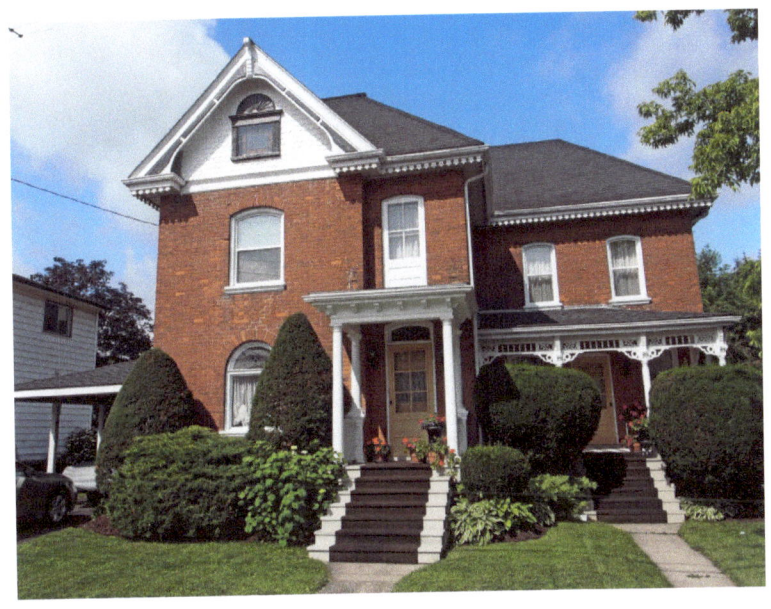

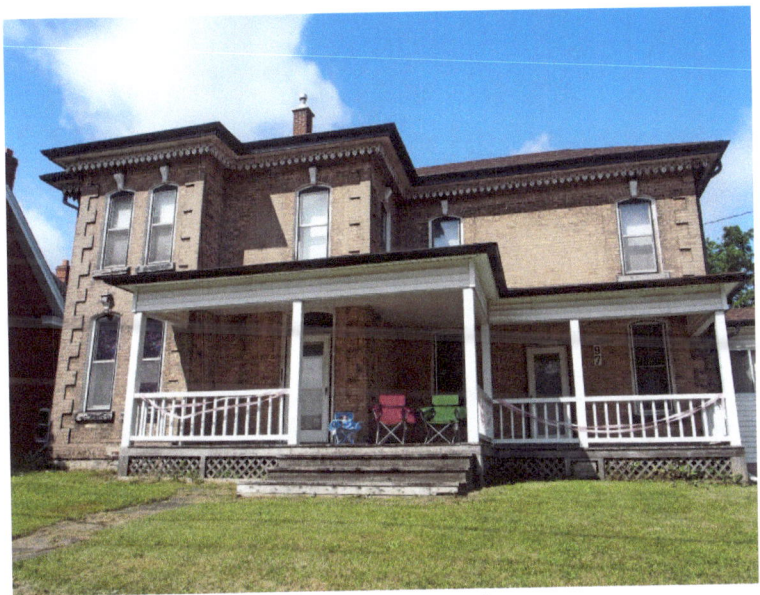

#97 – corner quoins

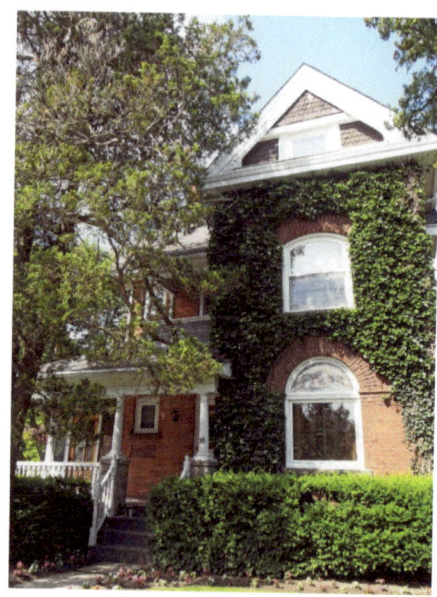

#95

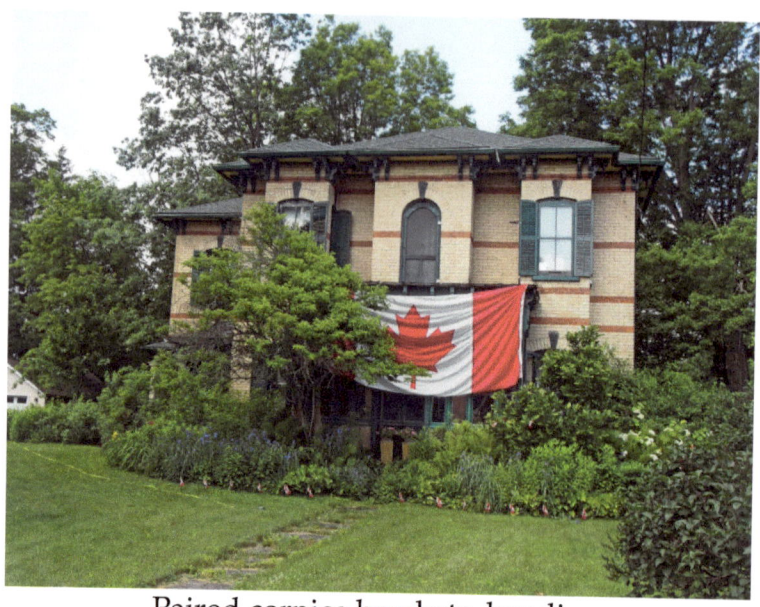

Paired cornice brackets, banding

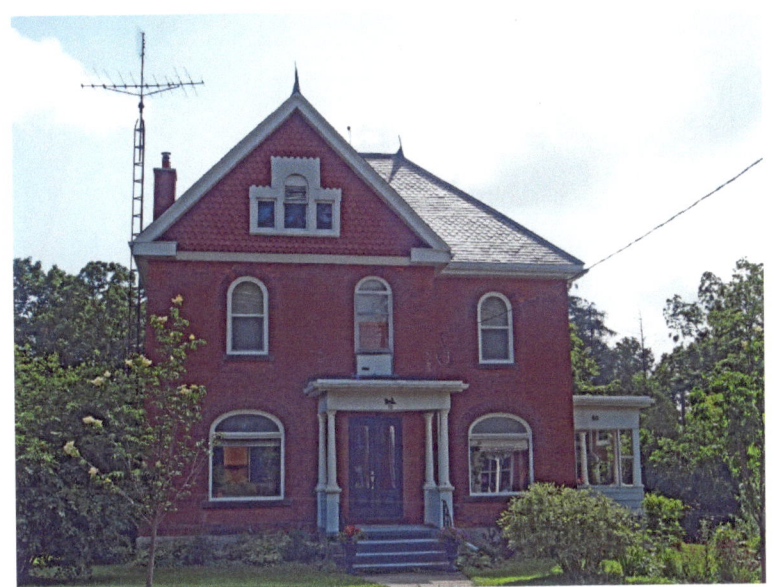

#80 – Palladian window, cornice return on gable

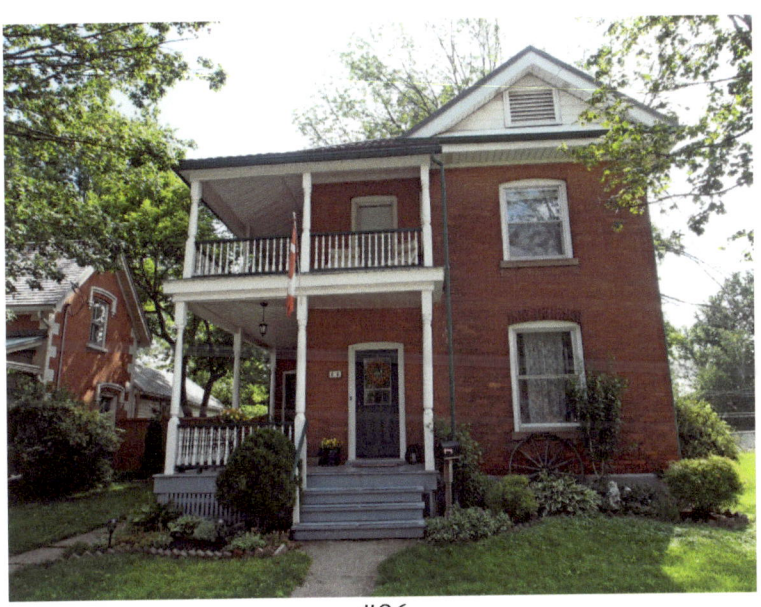

#86

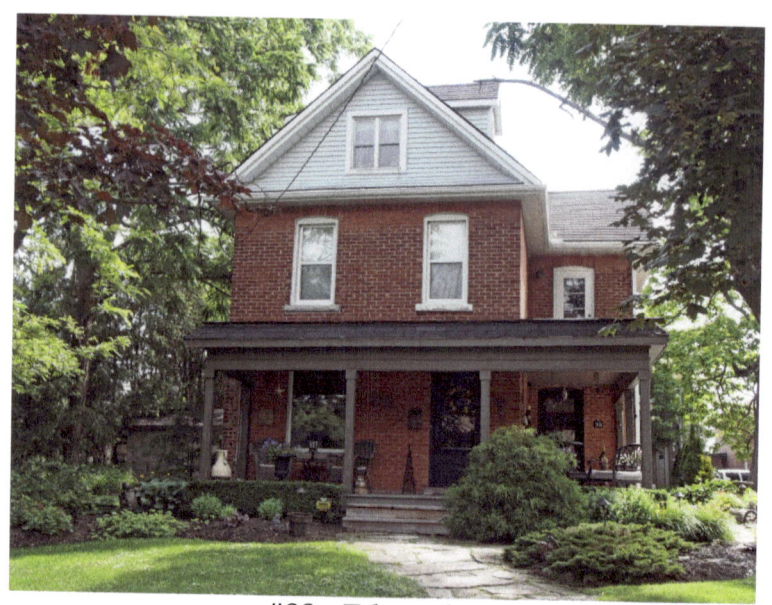

#98 - Edwardian

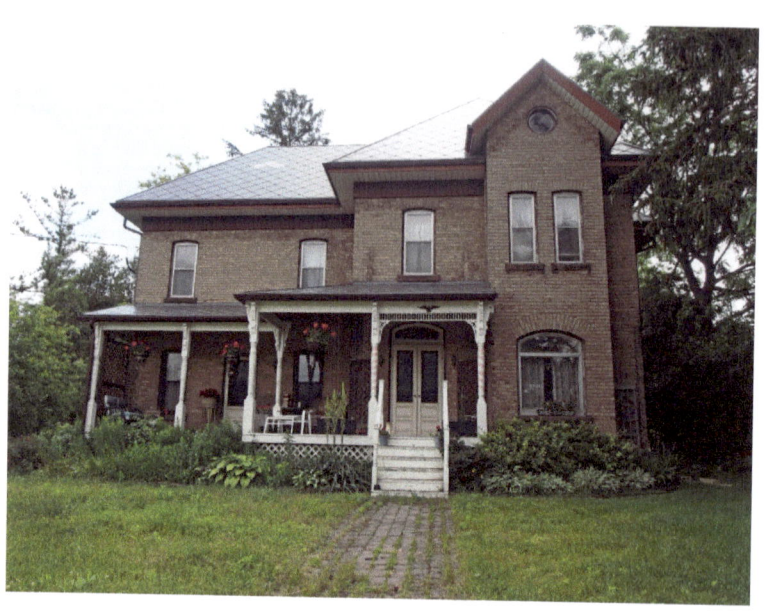

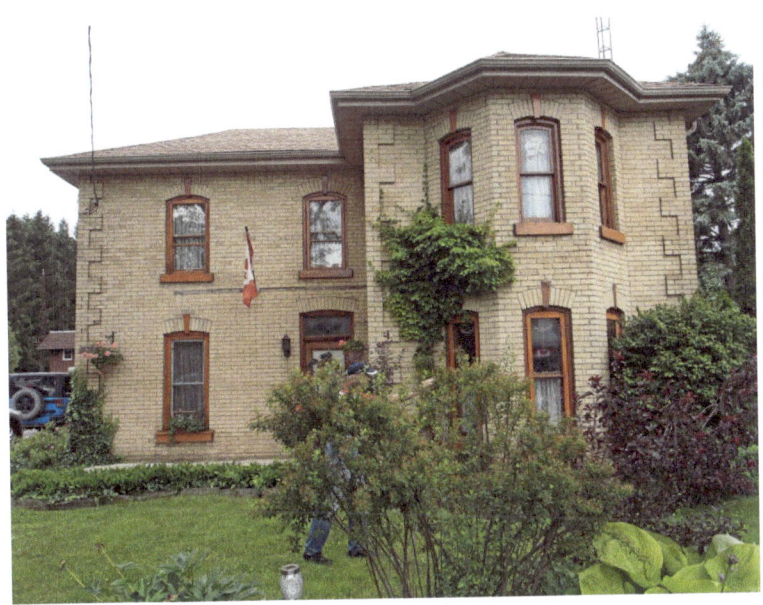

Corner quoins

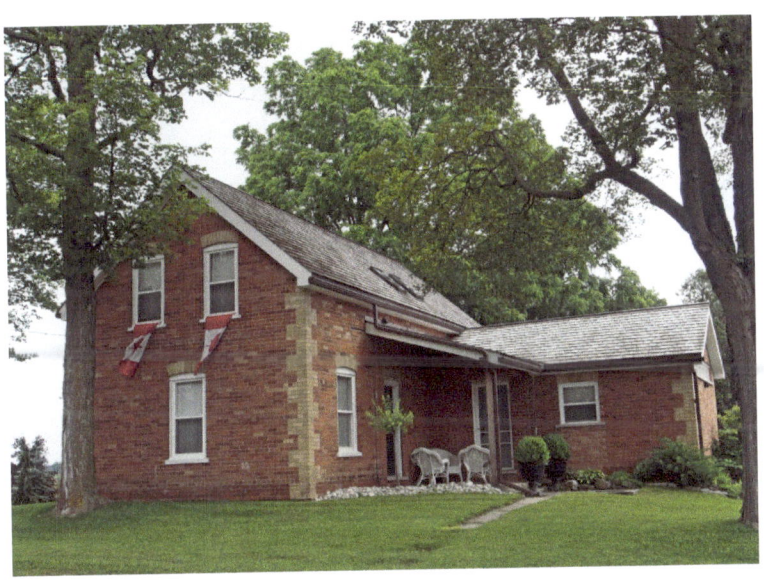

Mountsberg

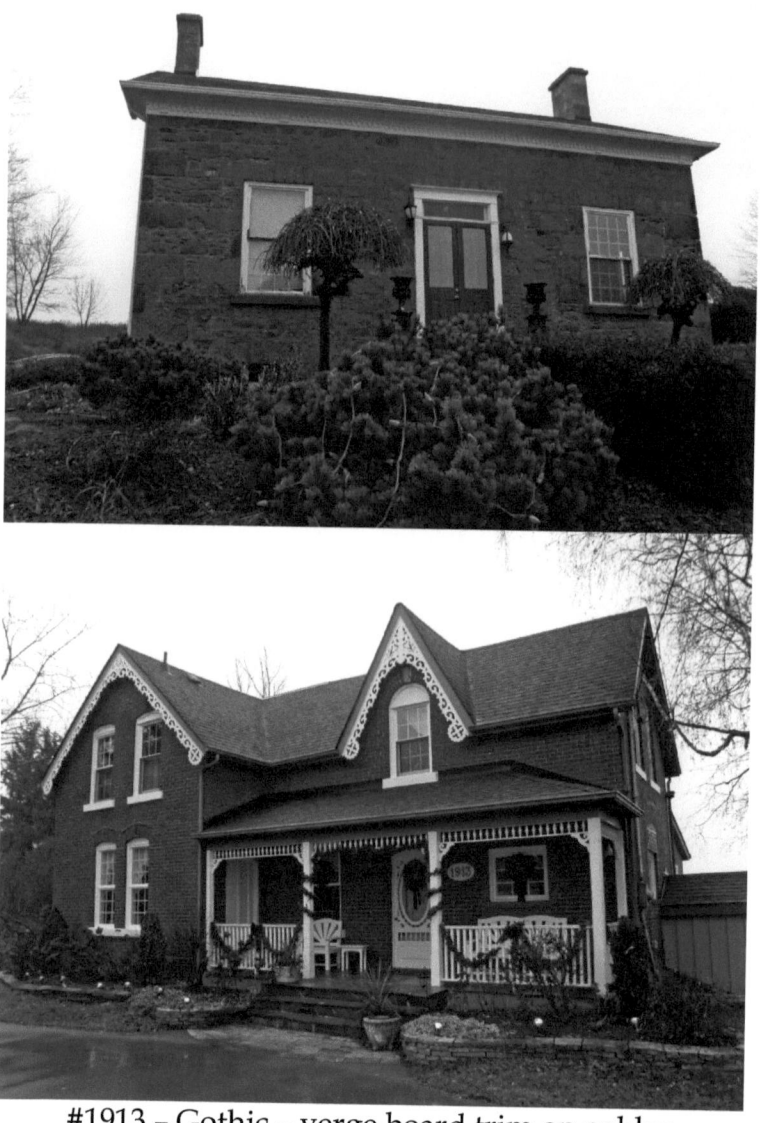

#1913 – Gothic – verge board trim on gables

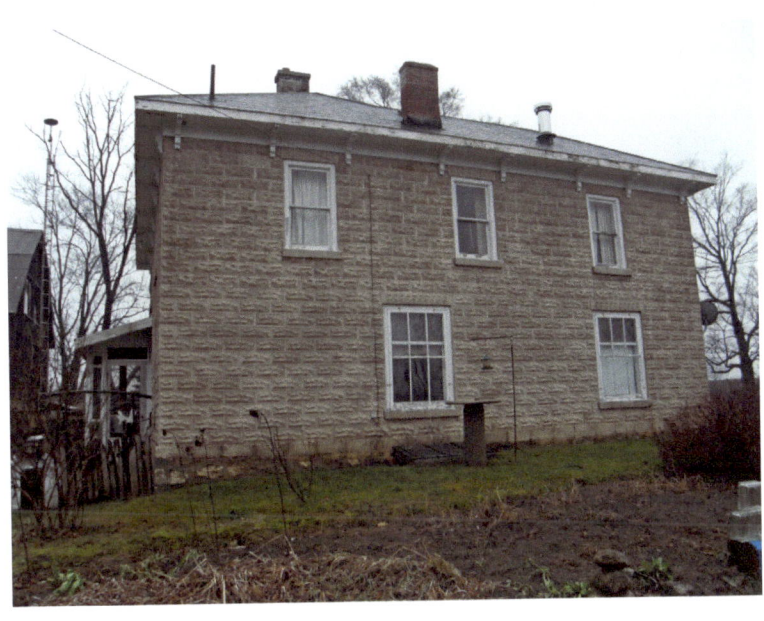
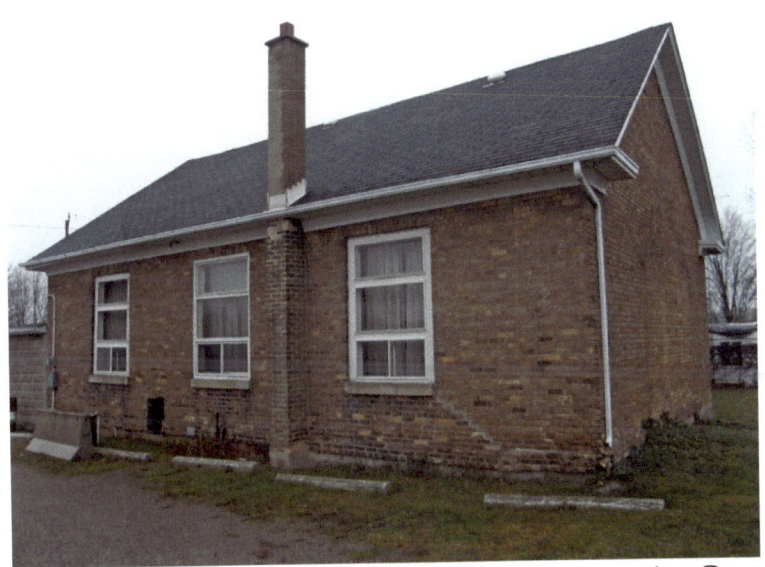

1866 School House – now Mountsberg Community Center

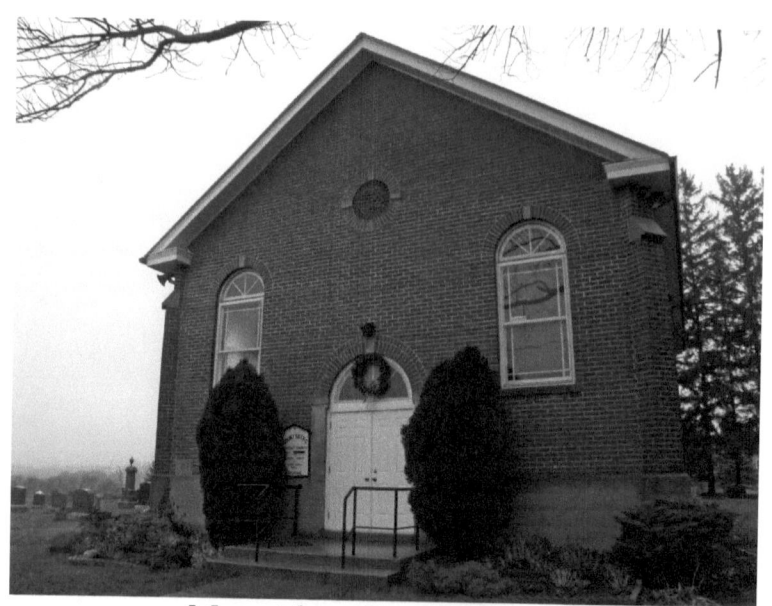
Mountsberg Baptist Church

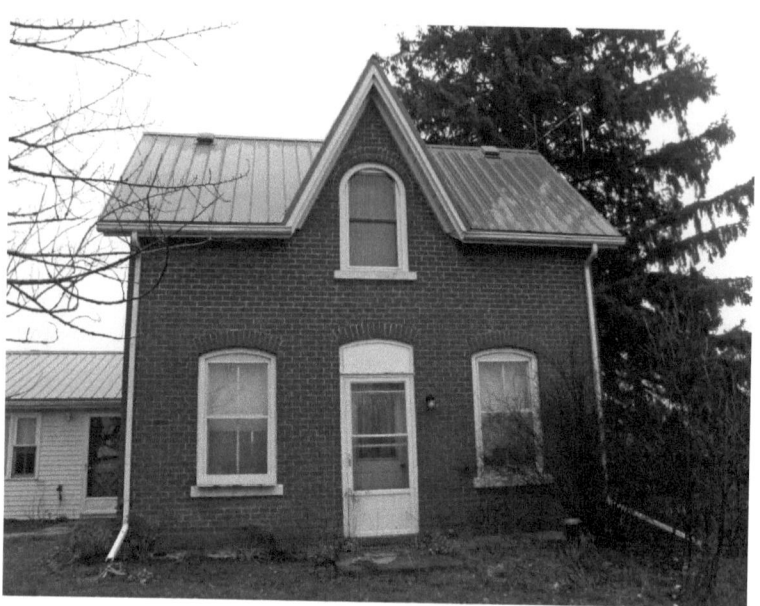
Gothic

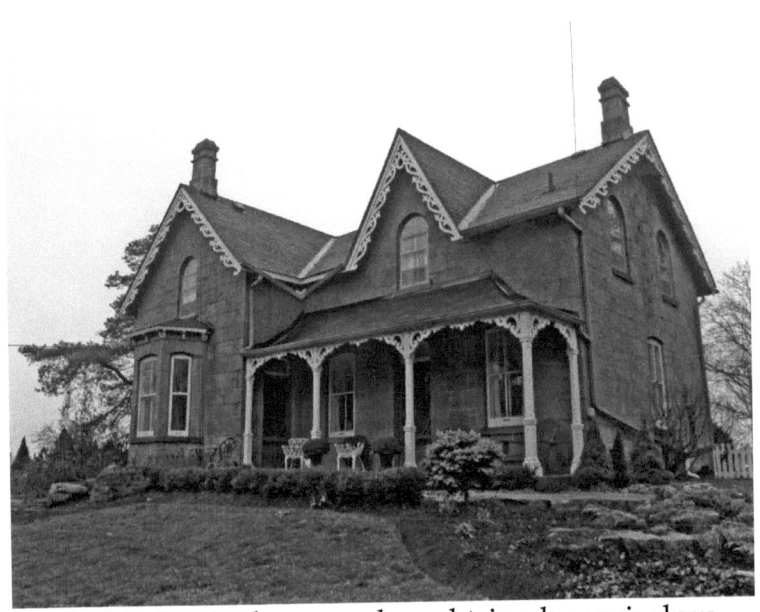

Gothic Revival – verge board trim, bay window

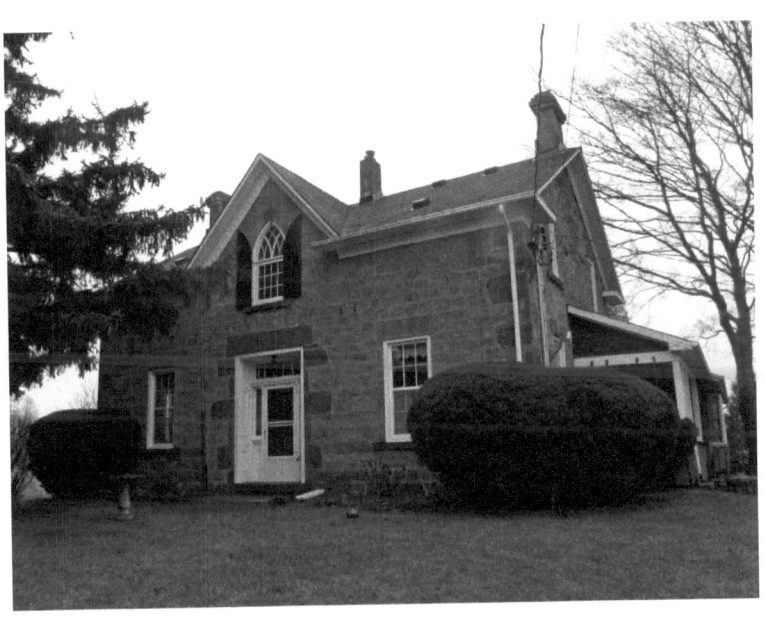

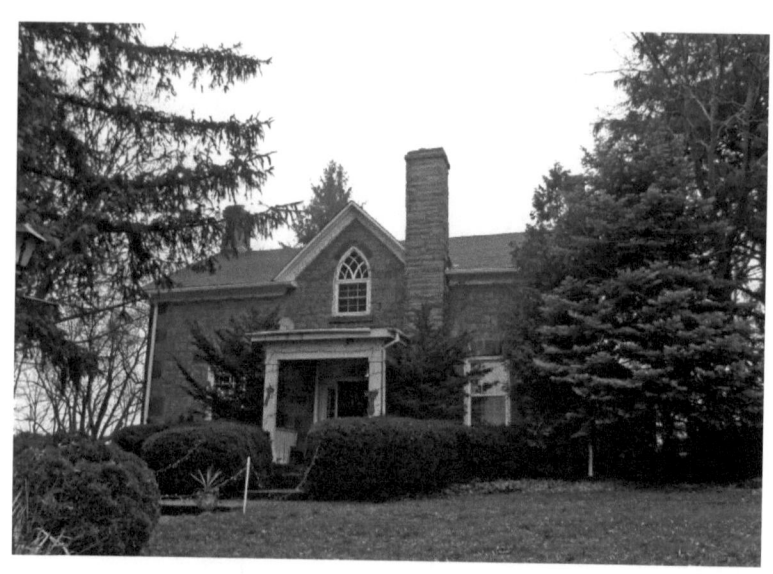

1866

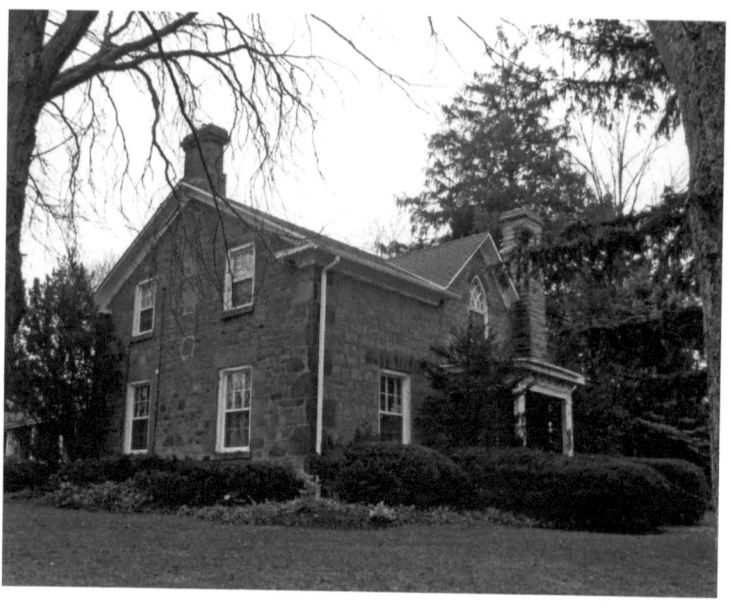

Puslinch

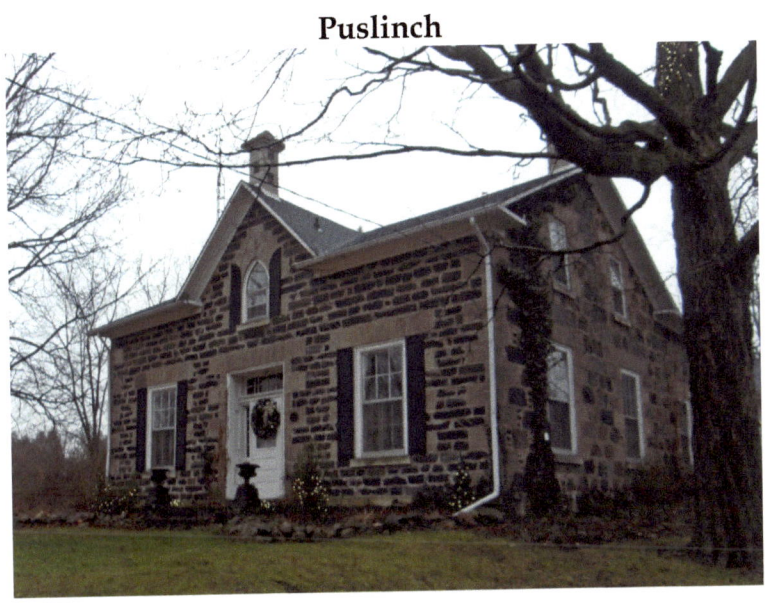

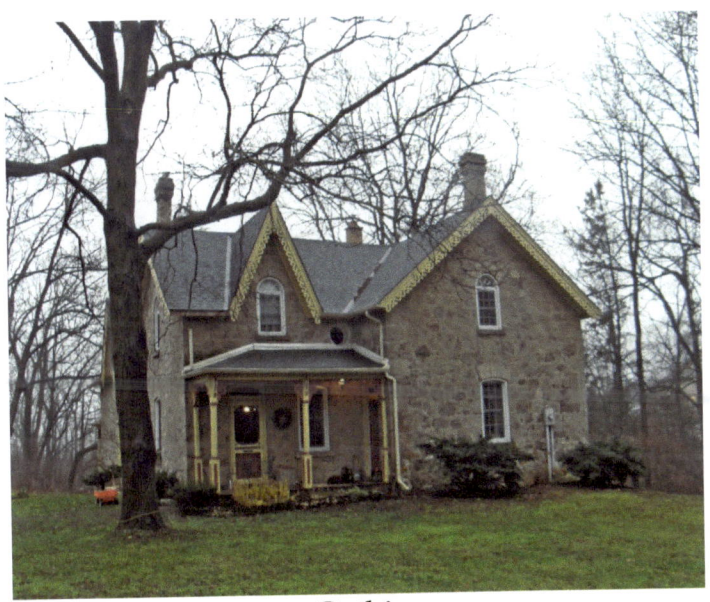

Gothic

Strabane

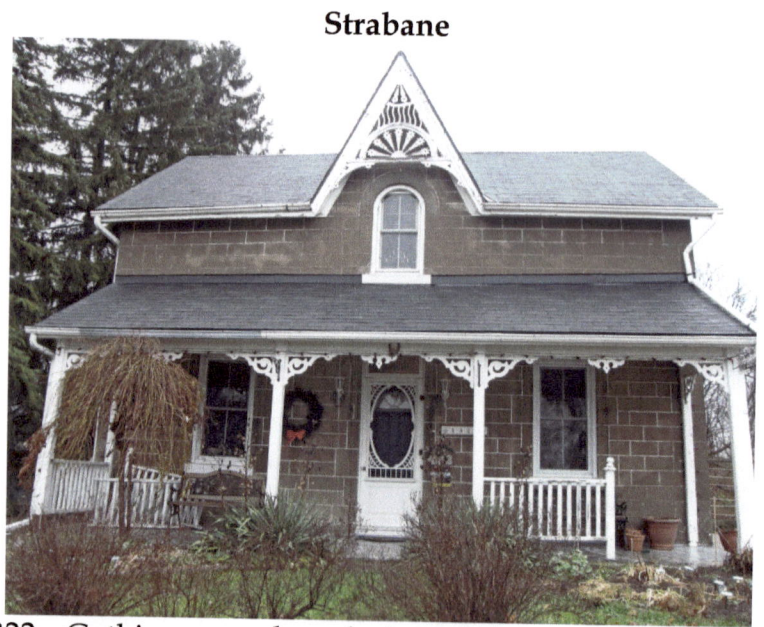

#1322 – Gothic – verge board trim and bric-a-brac on veranda

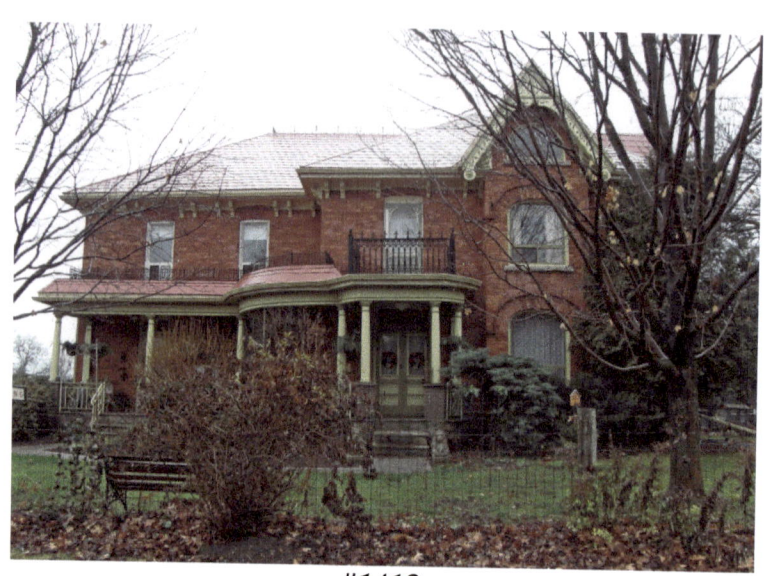

#1413

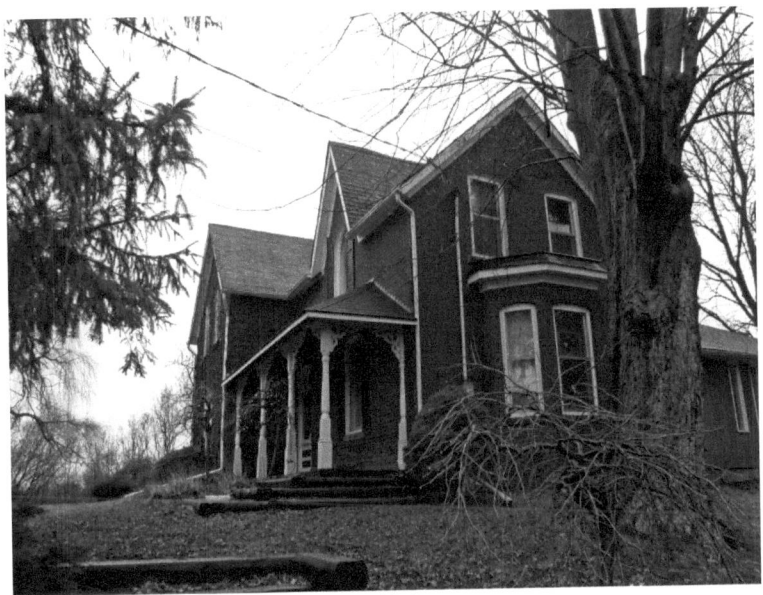

1436

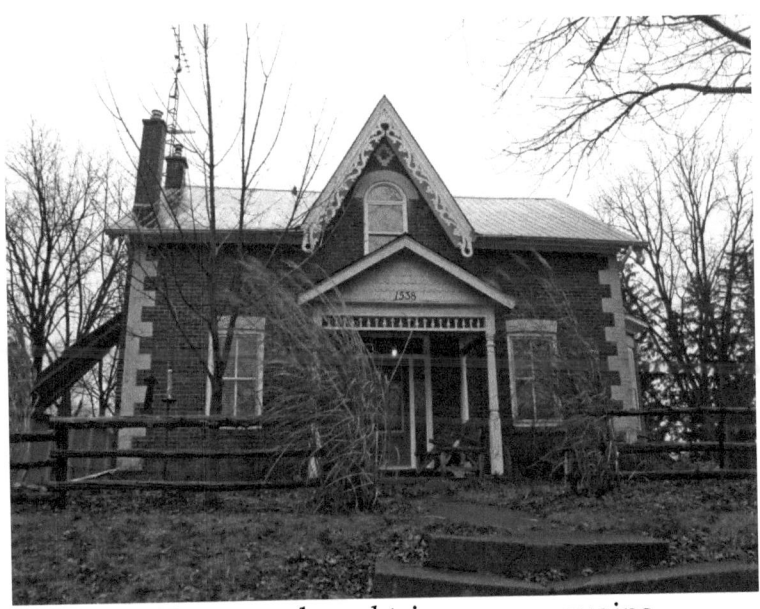

1538 – verge board trim, corner quoins

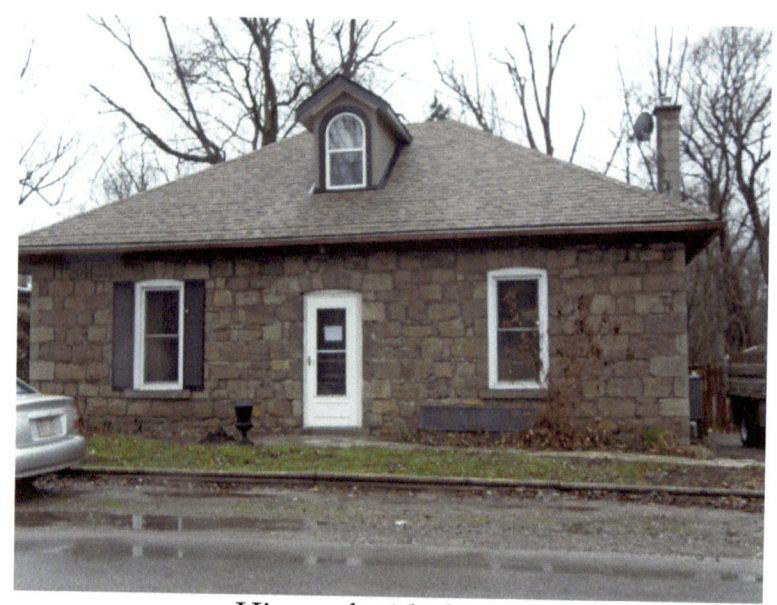

Hip roof with dormer

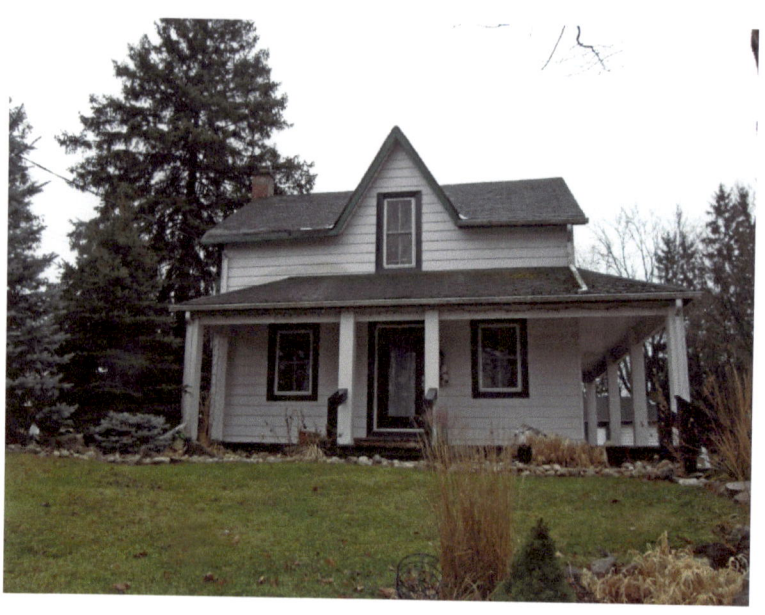

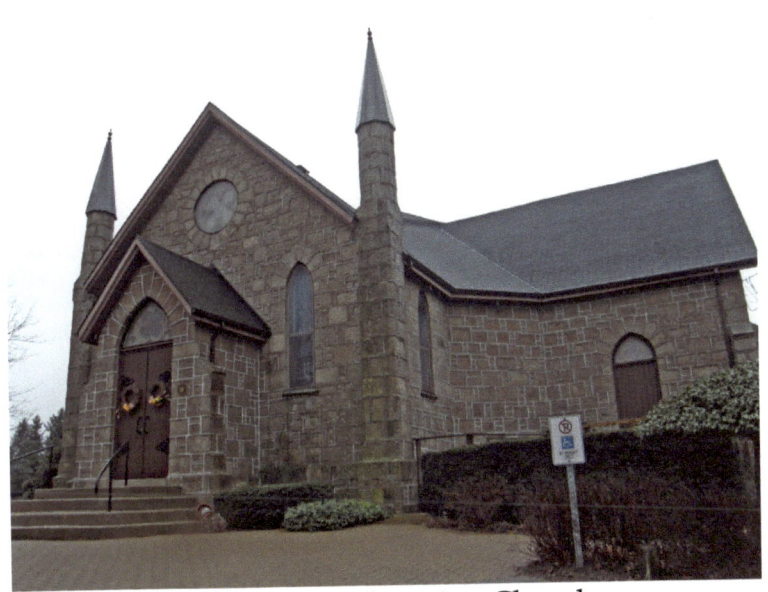

Strabane Presbyterian Church

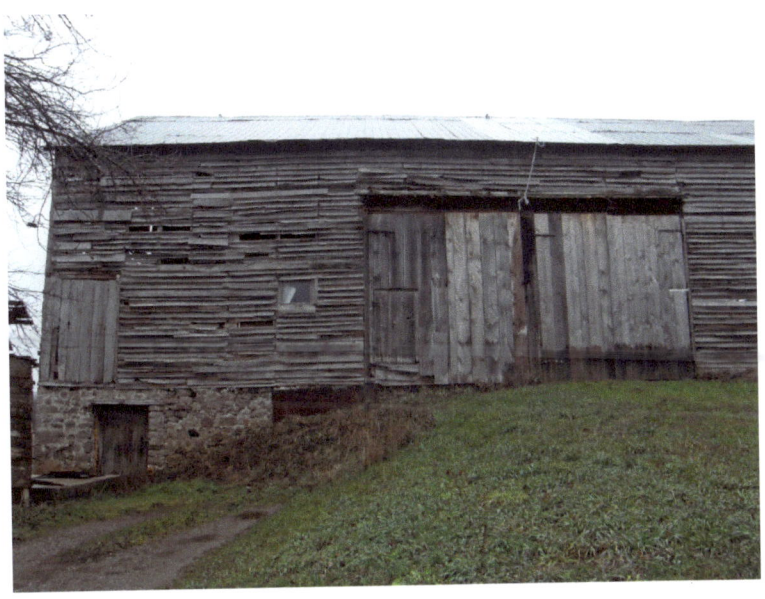

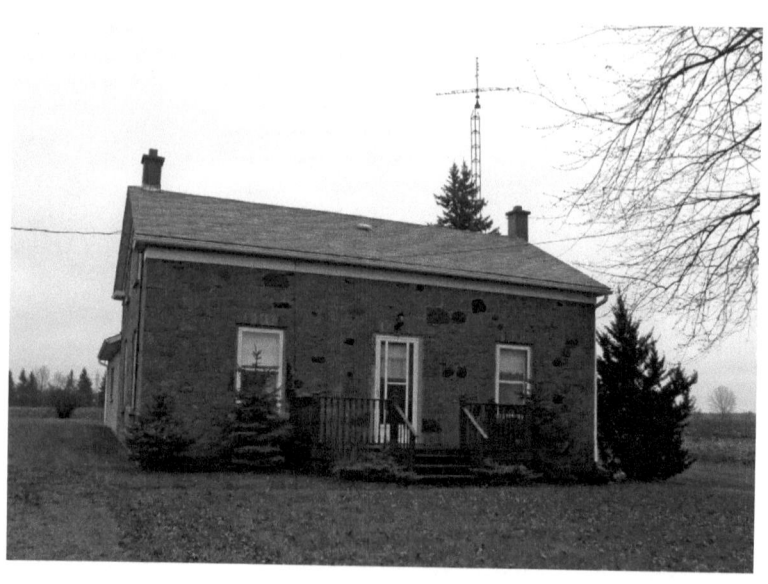

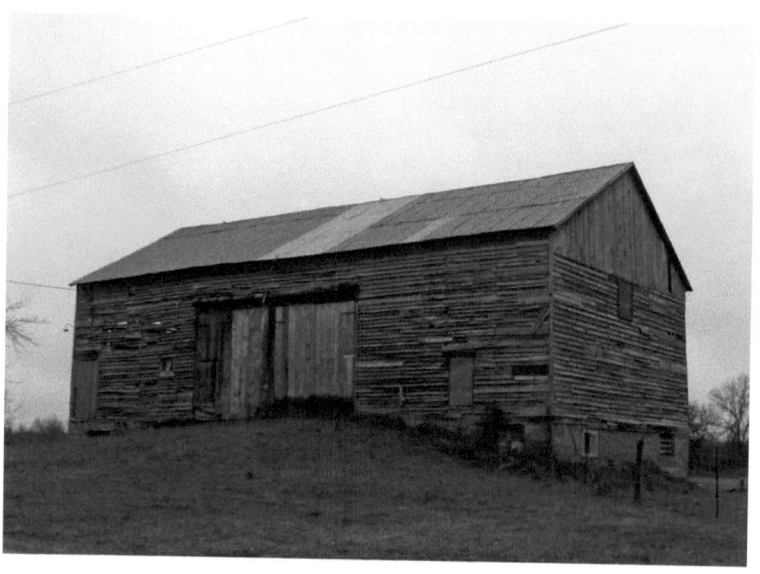

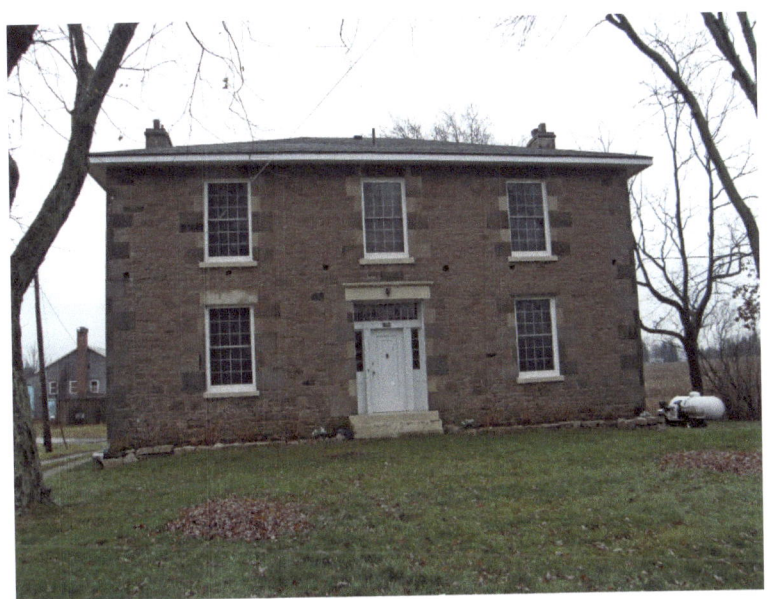

1754

West Flamborough

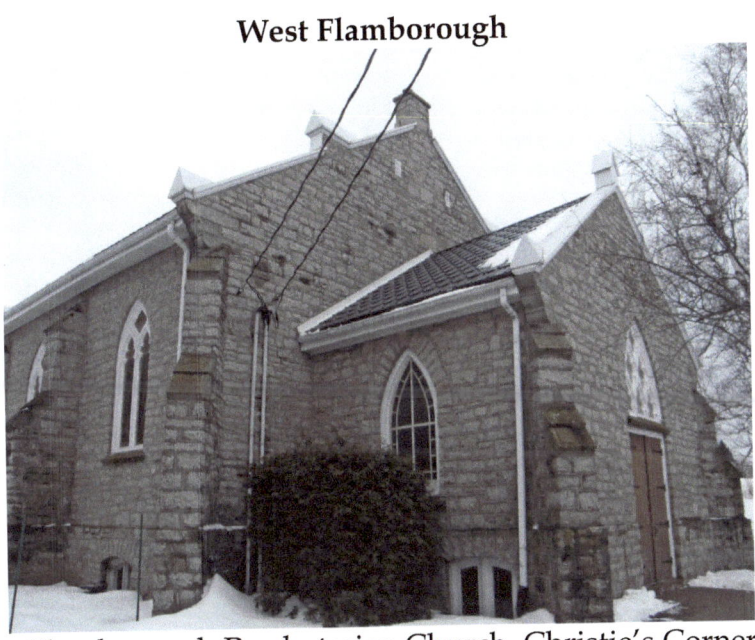

West Flamborough Presbyterian Church, Christie's Corners – built in 1866 – buttresses, lancet windows

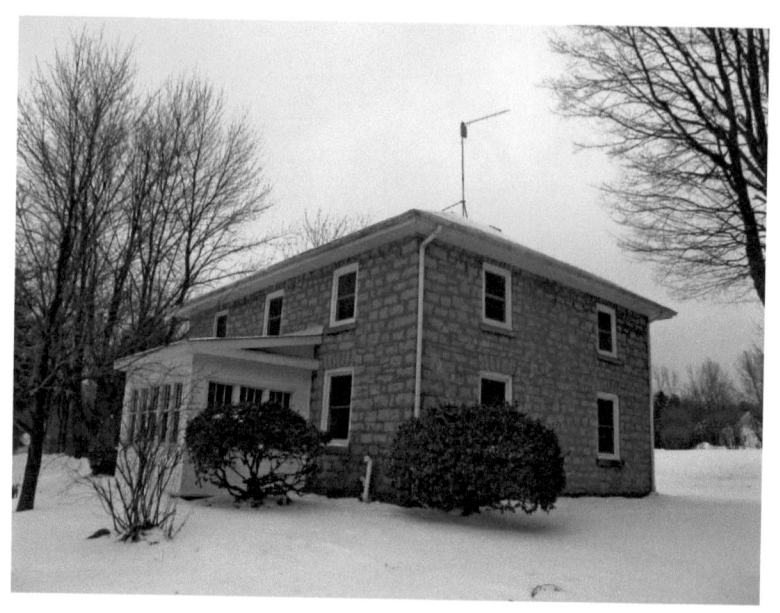

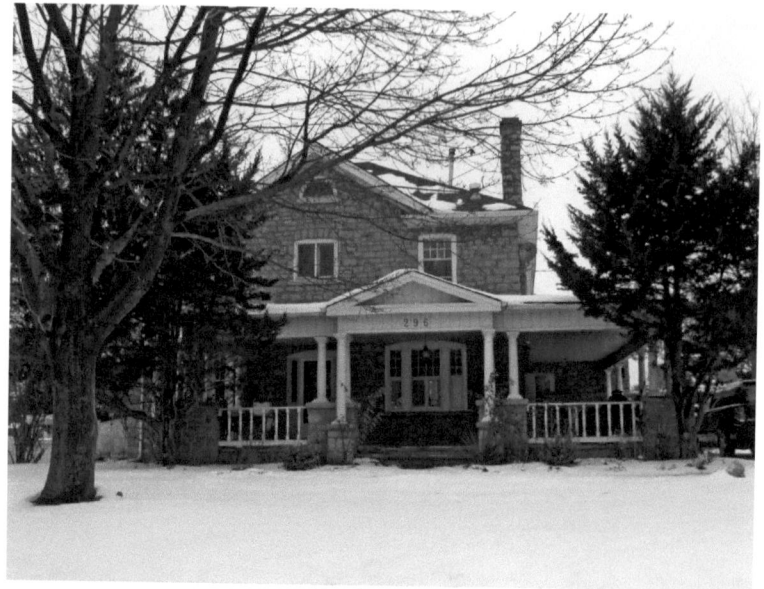

Pediment

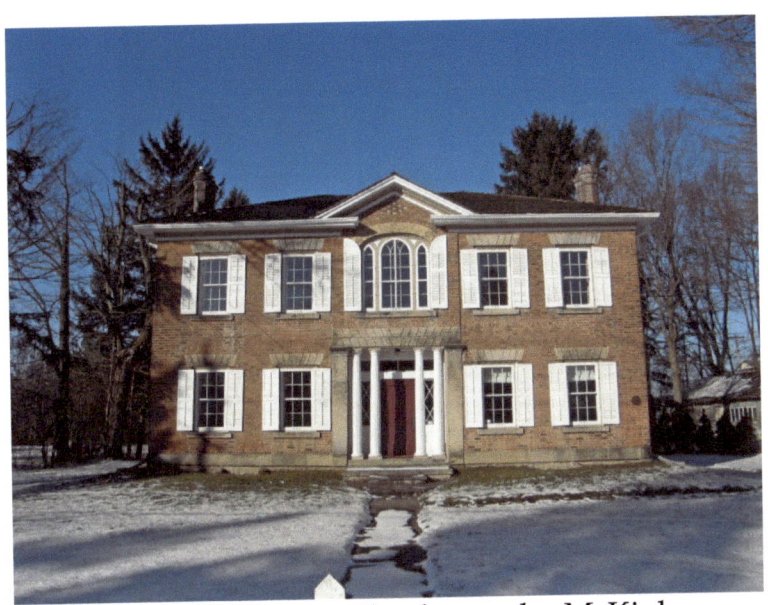

252 Highway 8, West Flamborough - McKinlay-McGinty House c. 1848 - Classical Revival architectural style

The front entrance is screened by four Tuscan wooden columns. The main door is flanked by pilasters of ashlar limestone set on a plinth and surmounted by a limestone lintel carved to simulate a rusticated voussoir. The door frame is flanked by sidelights with a four-light transom above. Above the entrance there is a Palladian-inspired window, set within an elliptical arch, with a central semi-circular headed window with gothic glazing bars, flanked by a pair of lancet windows showing the growing influence of the Picturesque and early Gothic Revival movement. Above this window is a recessed yellow brick lozenge pattern detail below a low gable with return eaves. The front windows have shutters and rusticated voussoirs.

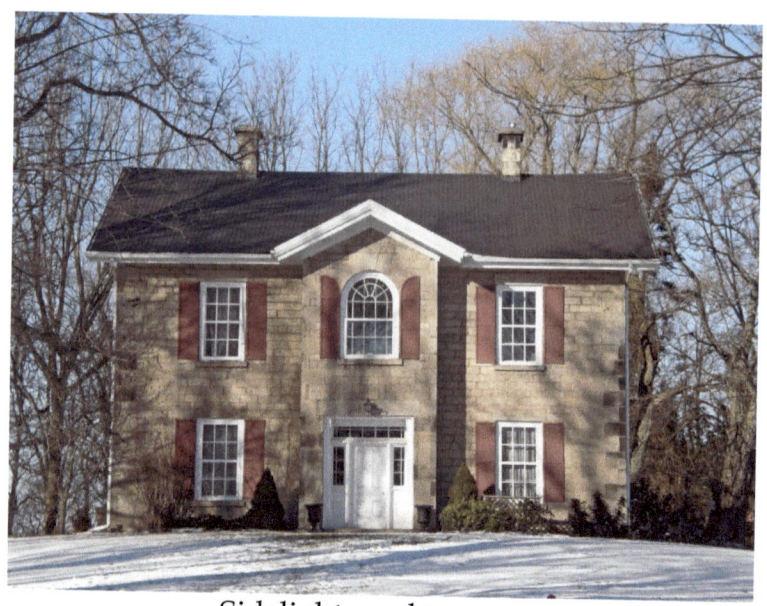

Sidelights and transom

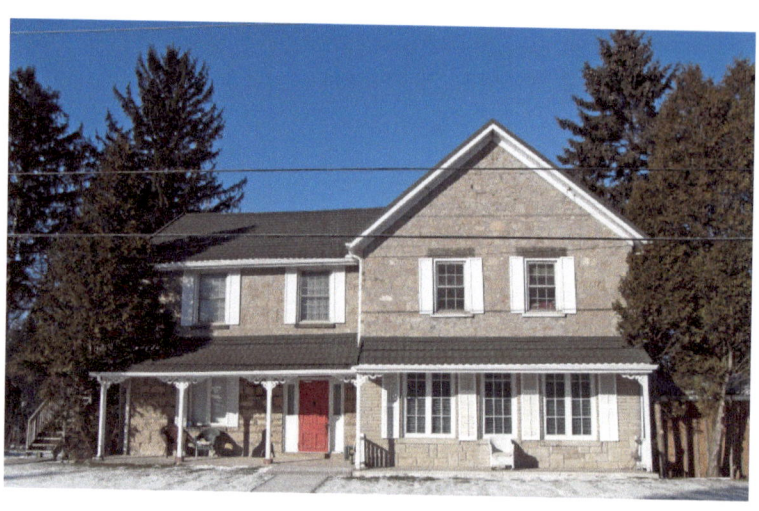

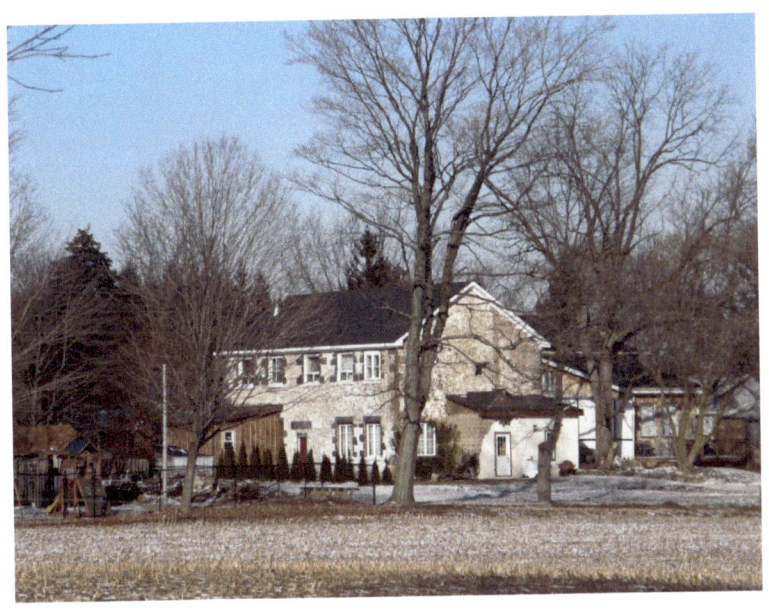

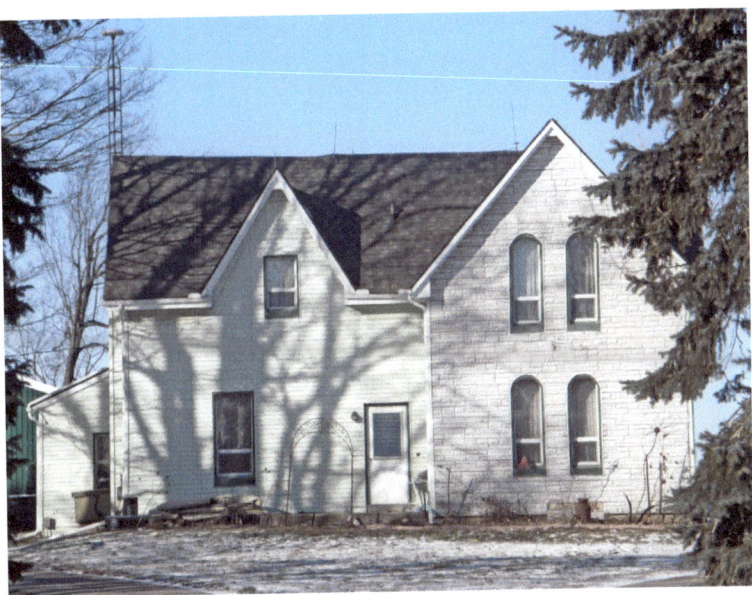

Gothic

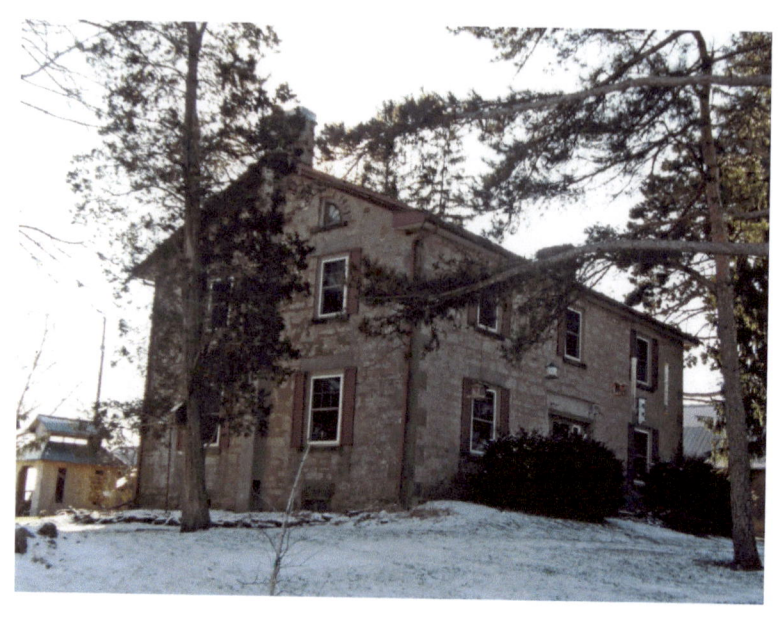

Bayvista Farm

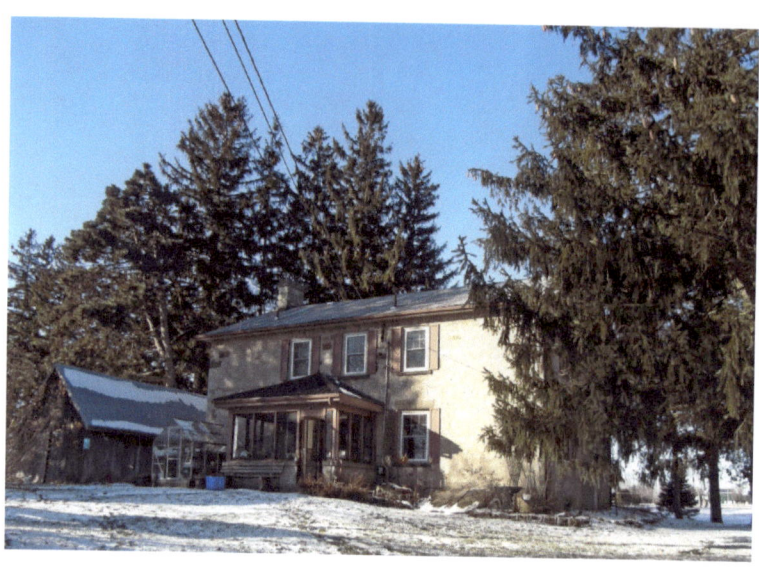

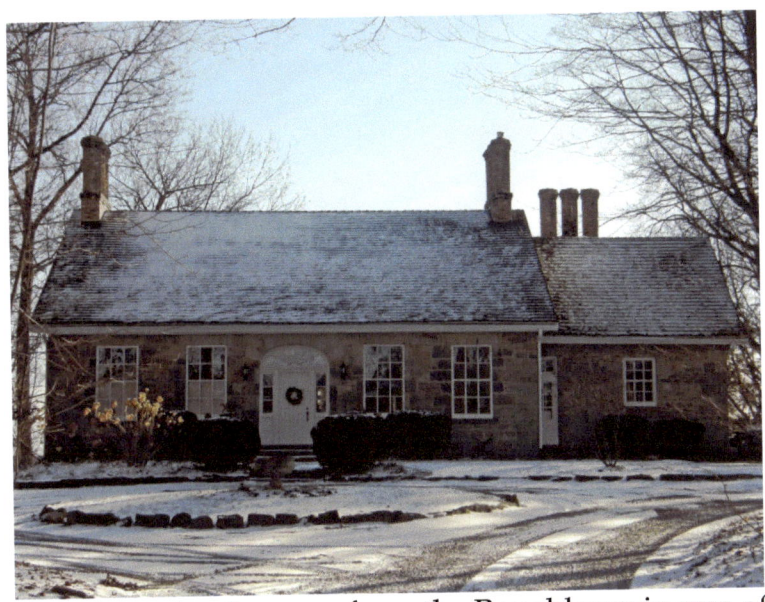

The Van Every family came from the Poughkeepsie area of the Mohawk Valley in New York and fought in the American Revolution as well as being part of Butler's Rangers during the War of 1812. For their efforts, they received 800 acres in East and West Flamborough upon which they built a frame house in the first decade of the nineteenth century. The house was enlarged and veneered in stone in the 1820s or 1830s. Three sets of triple chimneys show the amount and size of the fireplaces inside. The façade has five bays; the central bay has a Neo-Classical front door, a regular six panel construction with the connecting panels on the top four panels creating a cross. The fanlight over the door is deeply recessed; muntins radiating from a solid block hold six individual pieces of glass. The door also has sidelights.

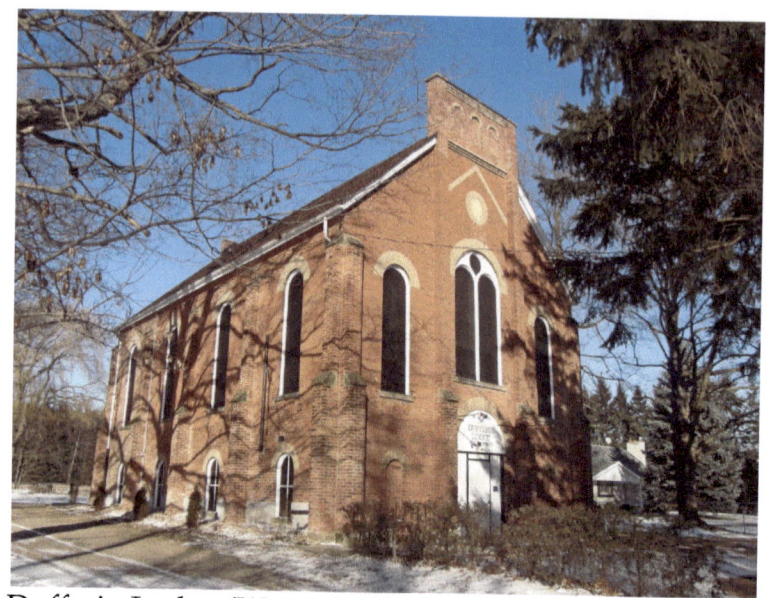

Dufferin Lodge (West Flamborough Methodist Church - A.D. 1879

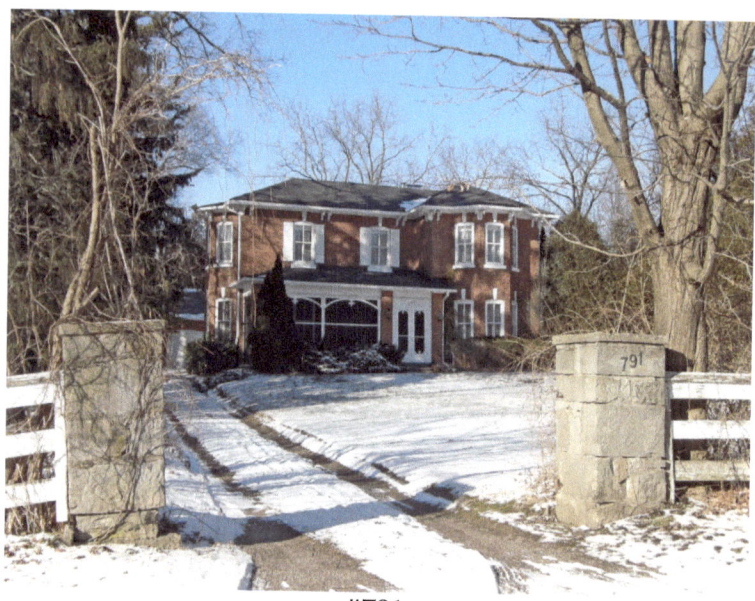

#791

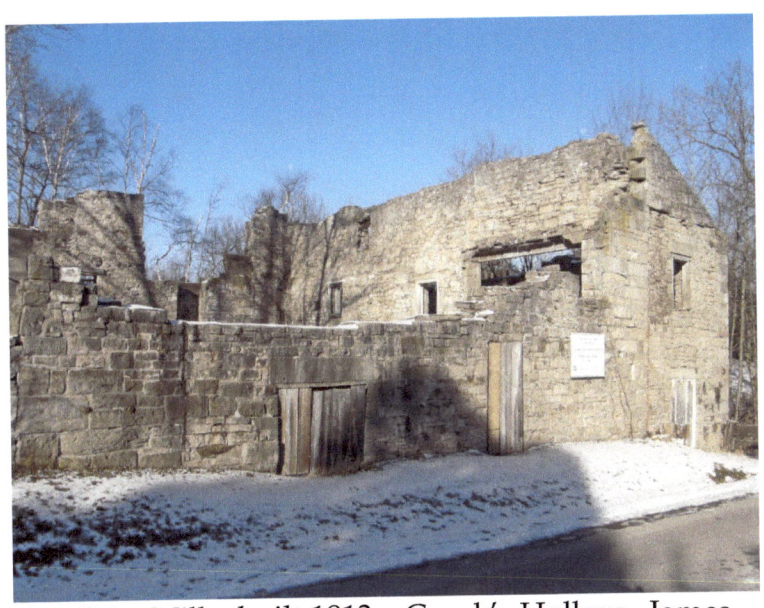

Darnley Grist Mill – built 1813 – Crook's Hollow - James Crook purchased four hundred acres of land on top of the Dundas escarpment in 1811. Within ten years he built this mill plus a number of other mills including the province's first paper mill which began operations in 1826. Crook's Hollow was the largest industrial center in Ontario in the 1820s.

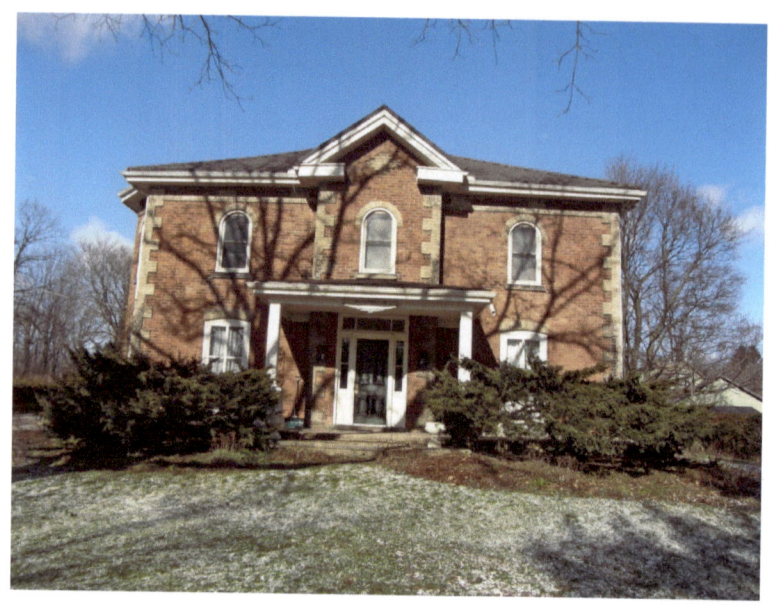

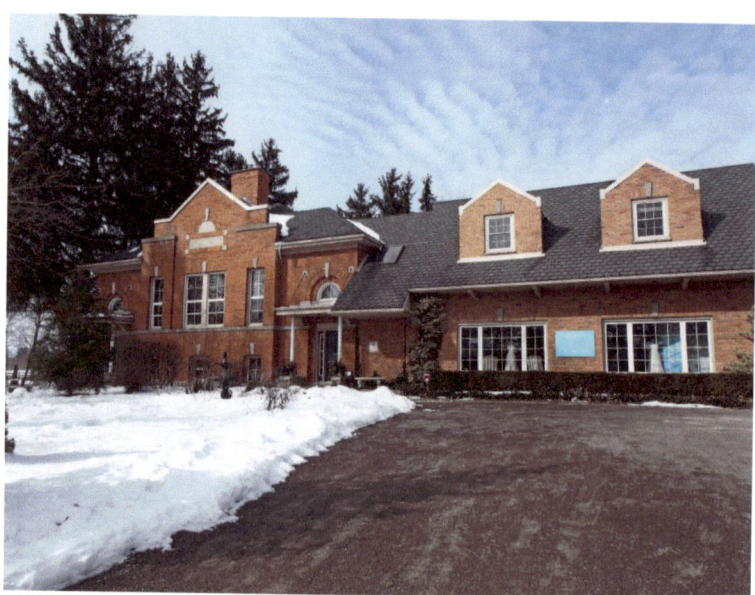

West Flamboro and Beverly – S.S. No. 7 School – 1915

Building Styles

Classical Revival, 1820-1860 – This style was an analytical, scientific, and dogmatic revival based on intensive studies of Greek and Roman buildings, concerned with the application of Greek plans and proportions to civic buildings. Schools, libraries, government offices, and most other civic buildings were built in the Classical Revival style. The white columned porches of the Classical Revival domestic buildings are identified with the mansions of wealthy land owners in Canada.

Edwardian, 1900-1930 – This style bridges the ornate and elaborate styles of the Victorian era and the simplified styles of the 20th century. Edwardian Classicism provided simple, balanced facades, simple rooflines, dormer windows, large front porches, and smooth brick surfaces. Voussoirs and keystones are used sparingly and are understated. Finials and cresting are absent. Cornice brackets and braces are block-like and openings have flat arches or plain stone lintels.

Georgian, before 1860 – This style began with the British King Georges in the 18th century. These buildings have balanced facades around a central door, medium-pitched gable roofs, and small paned windows.

Gothic Revival, 1830-1890 – These decorative buildings have sharply-pitched gables with highly detailed verge boards, pointed-arch window openings, and dichromatic brickwork. It is a common style in Ontario.

Italianate, 1850-1900 – A two story rectangular building with a mild hip roof, a projecting frontispiece, and generous eaves with ornate cornice brackets was the basis of the style; often there are large sash windows, quoins, ornate detailing on the windows, belvederes and wraparound verandahs. Italianate commercial buildings often have cast iron cresting and elegant window surrounds.

Second Empire, 1860-1880 – The mansard roof is the most noteworthy feature of this style and is evidence of the French origins. Projecting central towers and one or two-story bays can also be present.

Other Books by Barbara Raue

Coins of Gold
Arrows, Indians and Love
The Life and Times of Barbara
The Cromwell Family Book
Laura Secord Discovered
Daddy Where Are You?

Montana Series
Book 1: Montana Dream
Book 2: Life on the Montana Frontier
Book 3: Montana to Boston and Back
Book 4: Montana Sons Go to War
Book 5: Montana Sons Return from War

Donaldson Series
Book 1: Rite of Passage
Book 2: Rite of Marriage

© 2022 by Barbara Raue - All the photos in this book have been taken with my cameras. I own the rights to them.

Barbara is The Authority on Saving Our History One Photo at a Time. She is pursuing her interest in photography and architecture by preserving a record through photos of old buildings from the 1800s and 1900s with their unique architecture. Enjoy the beautiful architecture in the comfort of your living room. Dream about what it was like in those by-gone days. Dream about what it was like to live in a mansion like one of those in this book.

Barbara Raue, a wife, mother and grandmother, is an avid reader and writer. She has researched and compiled several family histories. In 2010, Barbara published her book "Coins of Gold," which celebrates the courageous life of her mother, May Todd. Barbara's second book is a historical fiction "Arrows, Indians and Love" which takes place in Boonesborough, Kentucky during the time of Daniel Boone. In 2013, Barbara published *The Cromwell Family Book* in which she traces her ancestry generations back into Great Britain. Her second novel is called *Laura Secord Discovered,* in which the story of Laura's service during the War of 1812 is shared. Barbara's memoir is titled *Daddy Where Are You?* It tells of her life growing up without a father. Five novels in the Montana Series have been published, *Montana Dream, Life on the Montana Frontier, Montana to Boston and Back, Montana Sons Go to War,* and *Montana Sons Return from War.* The Donaldson series of two novels is available: *Rite of Passage* and *Rite of Marriage.*

This is a link to Barbara's website to view all of her books
http://barbararaue.ca